D1648097

ISBN: 978-1-54397-615-1

Forward

Memories can be a tricky thing. They can paint a picture of the past that one remembers with nostalgia, or dread. Sometimes memories can be deceptive, too. They can allow us to remember things the way we *thought* they happened, or in a way that doesn't really represent what exactly happened. However, when it comes to Christy DePriest Wright, every memory represented here is exactly how I remember her.

I remember when Christy first came into my life, she was in eighth grade and I was in sixth grade, she was the new girl at church. My first memory of Christy is how cool I thought she was because there was a picture in our local paper of her, standing with essay in hand, surrounded by supporters for an essay she wrote in middle school. I thought she was such a cool person, because she had her picture in the paper. But then I got to actually *know* Christy DePriest.

I remember when we really got to know each other—it was the summer before my freshman year of high school and she was going to be a junior. We were teamed up during that summer to coach t-ball for our local recreation center, and because she was *so cool* and had a car, she was my ride to work. It was that summer that I got to know her smile, her laugh, and her genuine goodness—all of which was Christy at the core. When you were around her, it was a guaranteed good time. She had a wonderful way of making everyone comfortable, even doing stupid, ridiculous things outside their comfort zone.

But, the good times and the fun we all shared, was not the priority for Christy. The reason she smiled, the reason she lived her life to the fullest enjoyment was because of what God had done for her.

I remember how she could talk to anyone, about anything. It was truly a gift— especially witnessed by someone who naturally is an introvert and terrible with small talk. She was a friend to everyone. Her personality permeated through every group she was a part of and she made everyone around feel welcomed.

When you read the words that follow this somewhat inadequate introduction to a wonderful person, you will be reading a real story. At times it may sound too good to be true—but trust me, it is not. Christy was as real as advertised in these pages and it wasn't because of who she was but, rather, because of whose she was.

When Karen approached me to work on this project with her a few years ago, I knew there was no reason to hesitate and say, "Yes." Having just secured a few co-writing contracts, at first the idea was for me to help Karen write the book. But I knew, deep down, that I could not do this story justice. This was Christy's story, and who better to tell that story than the best friend she ever had? No amount of word-smithing on my part would have gotten this story to the awesome project that it became. My hats off to Karen, not just for taking on a task that would paralyze most—she attacked this with the heart of a champion—but for raising the daughter she did.

At the end of the day, I know my life is different because I was a friend to Christy Lynn DePriest. She truly was a leader in our circle of friends, and a true example of what Paul wrote in Philippians 1:21, "For to me to live as Christ and to die is gain." She was an infectious person. And, I'm glad to have known her and had just a small part to play in telling her story.

—A.J. Reilly
Riverview, MI
2019

Preface

As my parents received news that they would be having a second child, they began pondering names for a girl. They wanted a name with meaning and decided on Christy Lynn DePriest. Christy means "Christ-bearer," and because they were dedicated to living for the Lord, they thought this would fit me perfectly. I was born May 24, 1985 in Dearborn, Michigan, to two proud parents. Twenty-one years later, I am doing my best to live a life that glorifies Christ. They joked with me about the meaning of my name often. It could have been awkward if I had not chosen to follow Christ!

My parents mean the absolute world to me. They amaze me more each day with their giving hearts, sweet spirits, and encouraging words. They have been happily married for twenty-four years and have given me the perfect example of a Christ-centered love that does not die. My mom has not worked a day since my older brother was born because they felt one parent should stay in the home to be there for their children. My father works for the power supplier, Detroit Edison, and is able to provide well for our family. The issue of a mother being both a friend and an authority figure was never a problem for my mother. I have confided in her with everything and truly feel as though she is my best friend. We laugh, cry, complain, and argue together but at the end of the day, we know our love for each other is strong.

My dad and I were not as close growing up. He was the authoritative parent exhibiting both control and warmth. For some reason he received the bad cop title while I was young. He was very serious and could not seem to relax and enjoy life. It bothered me that he did not like to have fun. Now that I am older, I see he did not have time to relax amongst the busy life he lived in order to provide for us. The respect I have for my dad is insurmountable. It brings tears to my eyes as I see the sacrifices he made in order to give me a better life. How dare I ask him to relax? My parents recently drove twelve hours to visit me here at Liberty University, and we had an amazing time together. They never fail to make me feel special. I love them with a love most have never felt. I talk to my parents at least once a day by phone and miss them more each day I am away. They have always been hard on me and held extremely high expectations. This has pushed me to succeed in all I do.

I learned how to walk a life pleasing to the Lord after carefully watching my parents. They gave me a Christ-like environment to grow and for that I am eternally grateful. There are countless lessons they have taught me but the most important is trust in God. This is the foundation a parent must give their children in order to produce Godly men and women. I appreciate the fact that my mom was always home and there for me when I needed her. She pushed me further than I thought I could be pushed and watched me grow. She stepped back and allowed me to fall and pick myself up many times. She was there to brush the dirt off once I stood up and encouraged me to keep going. My dad is an amazing man. He attempts to present himself in an intimidating manor but he cannot

fool me. There is nothing but a loving, gentle,

warm Teddy Bear behind the serious face and

mustache.

I do not regret a thing about my

childhood or the way my parents raised me.

There are few things I may disagree with but I

cannot change them, so why ponder them? One

of my favorite memories of growing up occurred

in middle school. My mom told me that she

thought I should run for Student Council

President. This was absurd to me seeing as I

was one of the shyest girls in my school. She

told me that it was an awesome opportunity and

I should at least try. So, in an attempt to please

her, I decided to run. We worked side by side for

weeks creating campaign posters, buttons, and

writing my speech. I practiced that speech for

days in front of my mom. She critiqued me until

it was perfect. Once Election Day arrived, she

was in the gymnasium front and center to

support me. I had never been more nervous in

my entire life. My speech went well; I was

applauded and later was named The Hoover

Middle School Student Council President. This

was the beginning of my self-confidence,

leadership skills, and drive to be somebody in

this world.

I will never forget the way my mom was

convinced that I would win. I thought she was

hilarious for believing in me. She continued

pushing me in the years to come and because of

her, I became the class president of my high

school twice, the band president, the honor

society president, and countless other titles.

When it became time to apply to colleges, she

helped me study for the ACT, proofread my applications, and prayed with me. I was accepted to my dream schools and can only give all the credit to her. She helped shape me into the woman of God I am today.

I am the middle child of two protective brothers. Joshua is twenty-four and Benjamin is sixteen. I have heard of the middle child syndrome but am not sure this affected me. I feel I had the perfect birth order because my older brother was the guinea pig and my little brother got away with too much. I feel I received the attention I deserved, the discipline I needed, and the teasing I could have done without. I love my brothers and miss them a great deal while I am away at school.

They try to act tough like my dad, but they, too, cannot fool me. I see the love they have for me when I come home for Christmas and they are excited to hug me. It is also quite apparent when they meet the new boyfriend and interrogate him with questions of his intentions with their "only sister."

I am currently dating the man of my dreams. He is everything I have prayed and dreamed for my entire life. We are talking about engagement but patiently waiting to get married until we are both finished with school. We have yet to have an argument and share the same passion for the lost world. This is my senior year at Liberty and I am thrilled to obtain my degree in Business Management in May.

Now that I have reached adulthood and am approaching graduation in a few months, parenting seems just around the corner. I can only hope that one day when God chooses to bless me with children, that I can be half the woman my mother is. I already see many similar traits in us. We both love to laugh and have fun. I see myself resembling her in the way I love other people. We know what the other is thinking before words are spoken. However, she is the most selfless person I know and I do not possess this quality. I struggle with putting myself first at times. I pray that with maturity, I will acquire this characteristic. I believe this was a key aspect of her wonderful example in motherhood.

The major difference between my mother and me is our outlook on foreign missions.

God has called me to a life of cross-cultural ministry, and I could not be more excited. However, my parents are not excited about the road I plan to take. Understandably, they worry about my safety, well-being, and finances. Their concern has been a negative impact on this decision for my life. It is scary for me to leave the comforts of America for the uncertainty of China. It is hard to find encouragement from friends, relatives, and even my own parents on the choice I have made to follow where Christ is leading me. This ought not to be. As a parent, I hope to encourage my children when they make great decisions for the Lord's work.

When I get married, I hope to have at least five children. My boyfriend and I joke around about having ten kids. We plan to get married in two years and eventually have five of our own and adopt five more from China where we plan to live. I love the idea of a large family. I spent many hours babysitting in my younger

years and enjoy the company of children. I have
great patience with them and earnestly look
forward to the day when I will have my own. I
pray that I will be successful in raising children
to fear and serve the Lord with their lives. Can
you imagine the work that can be accomplished
by a family of twelve on the mission field? What
an example this would set. The largest obstacle
with this dream is finances. However, nothing is
too hard or big for our God. If ten kids are in
the future for me then God will make a way.

Learning about Jesus and being involved
in church had everything to do with my
upbringing. The majority of my life was spent in
Sunday School, Vacation Bible School, Junior
Church, Youth Group, Church Camp, missions
trips, and so much more. While I was
encouraged to attend church, it was never

forced on me. My parents encouraged me to find my own path. I was allowed to attend other churches, research other religions, and find my personal worldview. I believe this is key in raising children. No individual wishes to be forced into something unwillingly. Too many parents take this route today and raise children who end up disliking church because it had a negative connotation from childhood. If they see that you enjoy reading your Bible and attending church, it will be much more desirable to them.

My parents are not perfect people but they are perfect for me. God knew exactly what I needed and guided them in each step of raising me. I hope that my gratefulness is reflected in my deep love for them. I pray on the day they leave this world to be with the Lord, that I have the strength to get through. At times, I wonder why God has blessed me with such a wonderful life. Often times, I feel guilty for taking these blessings for granted. Many others were raised in abusive or unloving homes. I hope to take the love I have been so richly given and share it with the world. My dream is to open an orphanage in China to share Christ's love with unwanted children of The Orient. The Bible says to whom much is given much is required. May the abundance of love I have been given from my parents overflow into those desperately searching for it.

~Christy DePriest

Our relationship is described here by Christy just as I remember it. As parents, we were concerned at the boldness Christy had taken on with her desire to one day live overseas. It was something I had no clue how to handle and her dad was more concerned than I was. Looking back and thinking about how confident Christy was in her decision and her great faith, we, too, should have trusted in the Lord more. Our faith should have been greater. It was decided to include this essay written by Christy while in college. It meant a great deal to us that she would write this with so much love and passion. Christy lived a life fully devoted to Christ and the words among the pages to follow have been penned straight from my heart.

This is the story of our beautiful, strong-willed child, Christy, who inspired many—including myself. A girl who had a huge passion for following Christ on a level I never expected. Her top priority in life was to shine Jesus and she did that through her smile and kindness. It was never difficult for Christy to strike up a conversation with anyone without them realizing she loved the Lord. Her effortless ability to share that love was always creative.

~Chapter One~

Things happen in our lives that remain embedded forever whether they are good memories or bad. The last day of 2009 will be one of the days I will reflect on as a day filled with more emotions than I could have ever imagined. We were being transported by ambulance, from Lynchburg General Hospital, to The University of Virginia in Charlottesville, Virginia, which was a ninety-minute drive. The journey was taken north, on US-29, through winding road with rolling hills. It was an overcast, chilly day with a few inches of freshly, fallen snow on the ground.

The tests results over the past five days were basically inconclusive and my daughter's level of pain was unmanageable, so the decision to transport her to a larger hospital was made. We were given the option of Duke University in North Carolina or The University of Virginia which was somewhat closer to Lynchburg where she and her husband, Corey, lived, so it became the obvious choice.

Five days earlier, Christy had been admitted to Lynchburg General Hospital with a fever and pain she could no longer tolerate. She had been put through an array of tests that only told us something was terribly wrong. We all came to our own conclusions as to what it could

be but deep in our hearts we were thinking the

same thoughts but never verbally expressed

them.

As a bed became available at The

University of Virginia Hospital, an ambulance

was waiting for us. Christy was heavily

medicated to help calm her as well as limit the

pain for the journey north. It was my mission to

be strong for Christy and keep her calm. She

was extremely anxious about where she was

going, as well as the pain she was experiencing.

I rode in the ambulance beside Christy

as our husbands followed behind in separate

vehicles. Christy held her stuffed bear that was

dressed as a doctor that she had received from

Corey. Although she was twenty years old, she

still needed something to hold onto and, also,

she needed her mom by her side. We were blessed to have a monitoring paramedic with us en route. She could see in Christy's eyes the apprehension of traveling to an unfamiliar place.

Trying to stay strong and in control was not an easy task for me. I was falling apart inside because this was all too big for me and every ounce of my being was consumed with a sense of the inability to comprehend it all. I wanted to flee from this horrible situation—but wasn't going anywhere; this was my beautiful daughter lying in the hospital bed. Something was terribly wrong and I could do nothing to remedy the circumstances that were placed before us.

When we arrived at the hospital, it was early evening, and I knew as we made our way down the corridor that the accommodations would not be quite the same as they were in Lynchburg. The hospital was big with long hallways and not quite as updated. Christy was placed in a semi-private room . . . and I could see she was ready to hyperventilate. She was so distressed, desiring solitude; I understood because Christy was quite a private person.

Once Christy was placed in her bed she was visited by many doctors and nurses. The holiday made it hard to have tests ordered right away and all the questions and examinations were taxing on her. The patient in the bed on the other side of the curtain was having issues and was loud, which escalated Christy's anxiousness. She began to cry which bothered her dad and husband to the point that it needed to be addressed to the staff. Jeff, being the protective father, chose to have a discussion with one of the resident doctors. He explained the situation kindly but firmly. Within a short amount of time, Christy was placed in a private room—never underestimate the power of a father when his daughter needs him. This was a special quarantined room for patients who were receiving radiation treatments that needed to be isolated. It was available at that moment and we were grateful it was given to my girl.

Whenever Christy's radiant blue eyes would well up with tears that slid down her cheeks into her long hair, my heart would be pierced with overwhelming sadness. My child was enduring more than I could imagine and watching it play out before me was hard to handle. Handling the pain of my children was always so much different than dealing with my own. Feeling so helpless at this point, not knowing where to turn, and the desperation to find a way to soothe my daughter's relentless pain became my top priority.

In the midst of this ordeal I felt it would be beneficial to journal and began writing the events of each day in a notebook. I had written down everything I could to look back on one day. I am glad that I decided to do that because it is not easy to remember the details of something that was such a painful experience. We most often remember the good things that happen, and many wonderful things would come from this story, which many would classify as a horrific tragedy. I prefer to look at all of it as teachable moments that drew me closer to God and strengthened my faith beyond what I ever thought was possible. I learned things through this trial I would have rather not been subjected to but saw the gracious mercy of

God at work.

~Chapter Two~

I was raised in a suburb just outside of
Detroit, Michigan, in a small three bedroom
house with a younger sister. We went to a small
church a few miles away every Sunday morning
and evening. My maternal and paternal
grandparents filled the hard wooden pews
alongside us each week. The church was small
and had no air conditioning, which taught us to
design fans out of our bulletins. The windows

would be opened on hot summer mornings, inviting the occasional bee to join us in worship. The weekly printed bulletin would then become a multi-purpose tool.

This was the only church I had ever attended and loved. It only held about one hundred and fifty people and we all knew each other very well. As families moved away and older people passed on, our congregation began to dwindle to less than fifty members. My parents realized it was time for them to find a new place of worship for our family, and we began to search. It didn't take long to find a place that suited us, and it was the church lead by my piano teachers' husband. The youth group was a reasonable size and we seemed to fit right in.

Christ with a Y

Not long after getting settled at this church, my piano teacher was going to be out of town for a few weeks. She asked me to play the organ for the Sunday morning service. I was a piano student, not an organ student, and as a fourteen-year-old girl, I did not willingly agree. She coached me on how to work the pedals, set the stops, and I did what I was asked to do. I'm sure this was God's plan, as a young boy just a few months older than me took notice of the new girl playing the hymns on the platform. He asked his friend sitting next to him if he knew me and that answer was, "yes." We were introduced and, after five years of dating, that boy later became my husband. Being so young, we grew apart many times throughout our dating season and dated other people, but knew we were chosen for each other by God.

Jeff only had his drivers permit a few months prior to meeting me, so everywhere we went, his mother would be in the car with us. It was a great day when he turned sixteen and could drive us to our destinations without supervision. Our dates usually consisted of driving around, a movie, and grabbing food. We went to all the youth activities at church surrounded by our friends which was always a great time. Jeff was involved with his high school track team; so much of our time was spent on chilly spring days at meets. He was a good athlete and held a record at his school until it recently closed. My high school was across town, where I was involved in the business program. Jeff graduated a year before I did and went away to college for one year. We did not do well apart from each other, so he came back and attended community college. After I graduated, I was working as an administrative assistant at a large corporation where I had worked as a co-op student. A few years later, Jeff was hired at our utility company as a power plant operator, and I took a position with an insurance agent who had been a teacher at the junior high school I attended.

We began our lives together living in a small apartment for six months in the early eighties, and then into a three bedroom home that was built by my uncle. This house was only two streets south of where I had grown up. Jeff and I decided I would stay at home to raise our family. Our budget was tight, but we had all we needed as a family.

Jeff worked long hours and took on all the over-time he could get to help us stay ahead.

His schedule was a swing shift, and most days he would work sixteen hours with ninety minutes of travel time. We didn't see him much, and when we did he was usually sleeping. I spent those long days playing many roles, but enjoyed doing that. I enjoyed finding things to do with the kids while Jeff was working or sleeping, but it was hard to keep them quiet on the days we stayed home. Jeff was a light sleeper and three kids were a challenge for me, but we survived. When we added a swimming pool to the backyard, things became very interesting as it was not an easy task to stop cannonballs and loud screams of joy.

Our three children were all born in the eighties, with our youngest making it into that decade by three days! There was a span of two and a half years between Joshua and Christy, and four and a half years between Christy and

Benjamin. They all were given blue eyes and

blonde hair with extremely different

personalities. Joshua was a happy little boy who

played well alone and was very content. Christy

was our child with an attitude early on, and

Benjamin was the child who had to explore and

make his own decisions rather than take parental

advice. As they grew, they changed in many

ways except, for the youngest. He made us

laugh, shake our heads and pray continually for

his safety.

~Chapter Three~

The night before we went to the hospital for Christy's delivery, I sat at the table writing all the ways to spell the name, if this baby would be a girl. We never knew what we were having until the moment the doctor delivered our children. For some reason I knew deep in my heart this baby was going to be a little girl. Each time I wrote this name out, I would just stare at the letters. Would I spell it with a "K,"

or a "C?" Should I end it in "-i," "-ie," or "-y"?
If I used a "K," we would have the same first
initial. It was such a big decision for me to
make. I finally chose CHRISTY because it
looked very soft and delicate on paper. I smiled
and knew this is how it would be spelled, and it
was settled. Christy Lynn would be the dainty
little name for our princess to be. The moment I
saw her face, her name fit her well. I loved my
brand new baby girl, who was perfect and our
second gift from God.

Christy Lynn was born on the morning
of May 24, 1985, with light, fuzzy hair all over
her perfect little head. She was our smallest
baby, weighing in at seven pounds, ten ounces,
and twenty inches long. She arrived at 8:31
a.m., and I remember hearing her cry as they

brought her near my face so I could kiss her. I thought about how small and beautiful she was as I watched the nurses assess her health and wrap her up in a blanket. She was handed to her dad, still crying, as he began to talk gently to her. Within a few short seconds, Christy was soothed and fell asleep. I knew that would be the beginning of a special relationship between a dad and his little girl. The bond was made before my eyes, and I melted with love watching them. Jeff would continue to be the one who would calm Christy in any situation that seemed to get the best of her for the rest of her life.

Christy was a sweet baby that slept through the night and took lengthy naps during the day. The only issue she had was the inability to keep her formula down. We were at the doctor's office frequently trying to find out the reason for the surge of unexpected regurgitation that stained any piece of fabric it infringed upon. After some testing she was found to have an immature sphincter that just needed time to develop. By the time she turned one, she was better, which made us all happier and much more relaxed.

I felt extremely blessed with our little family of four, after overalls and baseball caps, I would be able to shop for dresses and bonnets. Christy was dressed in many things made of satin and lace. I was always dressing her in outfits, as if she were born a century before. As soon as she had enough hair on her head, she had braids and bows to match her outfits. As she grew older, she never wiggled away from me when I brushed her hair and pulled it back. I

loved to sew and made an array of her clothes
which were unique and specially styled. She
was my little doll and I loved every minute of it.
I vowed to stop dressing her my way when she
began to tell me enough was enough. My mom
dressed me in her style, and how I disliked that
as I had reached a certain age. Once I asked my
mom to take me shopping so I could choose my
own clothes; she did, and I wanted to do the
same for Christy. I appreciated that my mom
respected my opinion and learned how
important that was in a mother/daughter
relationship.

Christy's personality developed as she
became a toddler and she was an emotional
roller coaster most days. It was hard to figure
her out, as she would be happy one minute and
then crying the next. I remember becoming very

aggravated over these moments because Josh

had never been this way. He was always happy

and sweet, which I never expected from a boy. I

often wondered how such a sweet baby girl

could have turned into such an unhappy toddler.

She was so sensitive to my words which created

anxiety in me, as I did not know how she would

respond to me. There were times she would

begin to cry or exhibit other explosions of

emotion that baffled me. I believed our child

was never going to be "a cup half full" kind of

girl during these years, but I set myself on a

path of making sure that changed. Some days

were more difficult than others, but parenting is

a continuing challenge, and I knew I would

endure.

When Christy turned three years old, we

decided to get her a bike with training wheels

and streamers. The morning of her birthday we surprised her with it, and her reaction caught us all completely off guard. We parked the purple and pink bike just outside the backdoor of our house and took her outside to see it. With big smiles on our faces and excitement building, we watched her look at it and begin to cry. She ran back into the house while we stood awestruck at her ungratefulness. All I could think of was that we were raising a spoiled little girl. It wouldn't be until later in her life that I would realize how difficult it was for Christy to receive things. She was designed to be a person who would have a huge yearning to give everything she had to those who were in need. Her heart was always about helping others and never about herself in any way. I would eventually see that she was unique in many ways and that God had given

her a desire to be selfless. As I reflect, I now
know that Christy's character was already
developing, and I feel remorse now for judging
her reaction so strongly that morning in May.

After Christy turned four, our youngest
child was on the way. He was born in
December, and Christy would nurture this little
boy from early on. She and Josh were happy
about the birth of Benjamin, but he would
eventually become that little guy who would get
into all of their things, and drive them crazy.
The difference in years between Josh and Ben
was seven, and between Christy and Ben was
four and a half. It would take a long time for the
boys to become close, but Christy loved both of
her brothers immensely. She was the big and
little sister and would be a bit motherly towards
both boys. Ben allowed Christy to be his

mentor, but Josh was not interested all of the time in Christy's life. He would later change and want to be involved in her life as they became adults.

During my pregnancy with Ben, my husband's grandfather was hospitalized, and a few weeks later he passed away. We did not allow Josh or Christy to attend the funeral given their ages, and not completely ready to have them exposed to a delicate subject. After things settled down, we noticed Christy having great separation anxiety and would not leave my side. She wouldn't stay with anyone, including my mom, whom she loved to be with. We began to have issues with her going to her Sunday School class or preschool where Jeff's mom taught. As we put it all together, we realized Christy associated the hospital with death and knew I would be going to the hospital soon to have our

baby. Once I returned home she was much

better and her anxiety slowly vanished. She

never went back to preschool, but everything

else went back to normal for her.

Christy became very close to her new

baby brother and was able to enjoy him as she

waited for her first day of kindergarten. She had

seven months with him before her afternoon

class would begin at the same school Joshua

attended. She helped with all the things that go

along with caring for a newborn, which I loved.

Ben was a big baby weighing more than the

other two, but Christy still held him whenever

she had the chance. She would just smile and

stare at him, sometimes singing him a song or

telling him a sweet story. Josh was great, too,

and helped with feedings but never diaper changes.

I didn't get a good amount of sleep when Ben was little, as he cried every night for hours and then contracted a virus at nine weeks old. He was hospitalized and several months later diagnosed with asthma. There were breathing treatments to be given every four hours which took forever to administer. It seemed my days and nights were consumed with taking care of him, but Christy and Josh were really wonderful and understanding most of the time.

Josh's bedroom was set up with bunk beds and Christy's with a twin bed. Christy begged us to put Ben's crib in her room so she could help care for him. Since there was so much crying going on with our baby boy, we decided it would be best for Christy to sleep in one of the bunk beds in Josh's room. They thought it was great and talked and giggled together every night at bedtime. It seemed this third child had taken over the house with all he needed, but it all worked out. Christy would eventually get her room all to herself, and Josh would never have his own again. I don't believe he ever got over that either.

~Chapter Four~

On Christy's first day of kindergarten, she wore a little white pinafore dress with light blue flowers that I had made for her. It came just below her knees and had a big bow in the back. She had her hair pulled back with a big white ribbon tied to the ponytail while the rest of her hair hung down to her waist. She had bangs that we curled a bit, and she was the cutest little thing as she walked through the door of her classroom that afternoon. She had

become friends with sisters of Josh's classmates

so she was not walking into a room filled with

strangers. She was excited for school and I do

not believe there was ever a day she did not

want to go unless she was sick.

Jeff and I remained in the same

community we were raised. Which in our day,

had an elementary school in just about every

neighborhood. There were five junior high

schools, three high schools, and a few private

schools. As people began to move elsewhere,

some of the schools were closed. We lived in

the area where I was raised, so our children

attended the same elementary school I did. It

was a small building but had excellent teachers

that cared about the students and our children

thrived there. Josh was seven years older than

Ben so they never went to school together. Christy and Ben only attended elementary school together, due to their age difference.

We enjoyed our time with our kids as they were growing up, and we were learning the differences between boys and girls. We played catch with Josh when he started playing little league baseball. He was well adapted to catching balls that were thrown hard and fast. Christy, on the other hand, was not accustomed to that but wanted so badly to be like her big brother. Her girlfriends were already playing softball, but she had not shown an interest in participating. She asked me to play catch with her one afternoon, and it proved to be a disaster as I threw her a ball a little harder than she was used to. Christy's face was the recipient rather than the glove she had recently received. Her lip swelled up and bled while she cried. I cried and

was so upset that I had hurt my girl. Whenever

my children were hurting, it hurt twice as much

inside of me. What made things worse was

when they tried to make me feel better letting

me know it was okay and that they would be

fine. Christy was always more concerned about

others than herself. Of course she hurt, but it

always seemed to bother her more to see others

suffering. Eventually, the swelling subsided and

she never asked me to play catch with her after

that incident; a wise decision on her part.

Christy was sick often while she was

young but nothing out of the ordinary. She had

the usual cold and sore throats, but the

chickenpox she contracted from her brother

were unbelievably awful. She was covered with

the little red blisters everywhere. I had begun

counting them and when I hit three hundred, I

just stopped. They were in her ears, her nose,

her mouth and all through her scalp. Her hair

was down to her waist and I was not able to get

a brush or comb through it. We braided her hair

in sections so she could lie in the bathtub to

soak without having to worry about it getting

tangled. Christy was very uncomfortable and

cranky during those two weeks. She survived

the ordeal and it left her very little scarring.

Christy had so many bouts with

tonsillitis that we were referred to a specialist

and it was decided that her tonsils and adenoids

needed to be removed. We were not sure about

having her go through this surgery but knew her

absences from school were adding up. Her

doctor visits were frequent enough to warrant

our decision to schedule the procedure. I believe she was ready for relief and did not seem to be against it either. On top of the tonsils and adenoids causing constant infections, Christy had begun to snore a little during the night. Her airway was slightly obstructed due to the small, inflamed organs lying in the back of her throat. Tonsils are part of the lymphatic system and play an important role in the human body. They act as a filter for bacteria and viruses and produce white blood cells along with antibodies. Tonsils also are the first line of defense for the immune system. It was not an easy decision to put her through the surgery—knowing that removing an organ that was meant to protect her might not be the best idea. The doctor assured us this was the best decision for Christy.

We went to the hospital early in the morning and Christy was braver than I had expected. I stayed with her until they wheeled her into the surgical area. Then, I waited in the waiting room until they came to get me when the surgery was finished. After a few hours, I was called to recovery where my little girl was thrashing around and choking. She was beginning to wake up from the anesthetic and something was clearly wrong. A vein had been nicked during the procedure and she was hemorrhaging. The staff assured me that she would be alright, but they would need to put her under anesthesia once again to cauterize the affected vein. I remember feeling helpless and scared but knew it had to be done. I stayed with her trying to calm her but was unable to as she was so uncomfortable.

After the second procedure was finished,
all was well, other than the pain of post surgery.
What was supposed to be outpatient surgery
turned into an inpatient stay. I stayed with
Christy all night and we were able to return
home the next morning. She loved ice cream
and popsicles, so life was good for the next few
days. Christy's voice had changed a little and
she healed just fine. As for the sore throats, they
still came but not as frequent as prior to the
surgery. The snoring had subsided as well.

Then there was the issue of Christy's
teeth as her adult ones grew in. Her baby teeth
were spaced perfectly but the permanent ones
were not so beautifully placed. Her top front
tooth was turned sideways and it bothered her so
much. She was teased about it at school, and it
made her cry almost every single day. We took

her to the dentist and asked about braces, so we were sent to an orthodontist. She was not quite old enough for any work to be started, but when we explained the constant teasing she received, they opted to start a treatment plan early for her. She was more than pleased to get going knowing her teeth would be straight. She endured the braces and all the adjustments that came with them. She had some oral surgery done, and her teeth were beautiful at the end of all her years in orthodontic care! She wore here retainer faithfully once she had her braces removed in constant worry the tooth would turn back. Christy's smile was always beautiful, and she made sure she used it to greet everyone.

~Chapter Five~

We always made sure to be very

involved in the lives of our children while they

were growing up. We attended all their events

and coached them when we could. Jeff was

involved with baseball and basketball and I

coached cheerleading. Before Josh and Christy

were old enough to participate in elementary

basketball and cheerleading, we were asked to

get involved. Josh went to the after school

basketball practices with Jeff and the
cheerleaders made Christy their mascot. Too
young as a first grader to belong to the cheer
team, she was so happy the girls had requested
she be part of the Holland Hurricanes
Cheerleaders. This allowed both of our kids to
be able to practice with the teams. For Christy,
learning all the cheers and dance routines was
lots of fun for her. She was good and was
outfitted with a little uniform that matched the
older girls. Christy wore a gold sweatshirt with
a green letter "H" on the front and a green and
gold pleated skirt, just like the older girls.
Christy was able to continue as a cheerleader
from elementary school all the way through
high school. She loved this sport as much as I
had growing up.

I went on all the field trips with them and was part of their classroom activities, always volunteering when their teachers asked for help. But, coaching cheerleading was my favorite way of being involved.

Christy was also an excellent swimmer, as were both boys. They all were on the swim team in middle school, getting up early most mornings for practice before school. Josh and Christy had no problems getting up while it was still dark, but Ben was absolutely terrible. He somehow made it there, but it was rough on us trying to get him to wake up.

The one common thread we all shared was music. Jeff and I both played the piano at a young age, though Jeff lost interest due to his strong desire to participate in sports. Josh and Christy took lessons and then went on to play other instruments. Ben never wanted to play the piano, but followed Josh in playing the trumpet. Josh made it through his freshman year of high school playing in marching band and Ben quit playing after middle school. Christy, on the other hand, loved the flute and took private lessons on top of being in band. She continued through her sophomore year playing in concert band and did a year with marching band. She had learned to play the piccolo as an eighth grader and played certain pieces on it. She was so involved with many school activities that she had to give something up. Eventually, Christy made the decision to discontinue band, putting her flute away. Although, the flute was not played in school, she continued to play solos in church and was active in the newly formed orchestra. I remember hearing her practice in her room while she sat on her bed making sure

every note was played correctly and beautifully.

Christy was a perfectionist in everything she

did, causing great anxiety most of the time, but

we usually talked through it and prayed many

times for peace. Her faith kept her well-

grounded in her teen years which was good for

this mom's heart.

  I found it very enjoyable to share my

love for music with my kids and I would expose

them to different genres. We would spend many

afternoons dancing in the living room and

falling on the floor laughing at our crazy moves.

It was the late eighties so the music was always

fun for dancing. All three kids grew to have a

love for all kinds of music, and Christy would

laugh telling people how often we had dance

parties in our living room.

Christy always found opportunities at school to participate in, and when we decided to attend a new church in the late nineties, she found exactly where her calling was. This church was much larger than the one we attended and there were many teens that took Christy right in. She enjoyed her new friends and quickly became part of the youth group. She eagerly waited for Sunday mornings to come so she could be with her new church family, but also to learn more about God's word. She attended every service and activity that was scheduled. Her Bible was filled with notes along the margins of pages, and the front and back covers as well. She had dates next to scriptures and little hearts by the ones she loved. She not only read her Bible but questioned everything and yearned constantly for more. I saw my daughter transforming into the most wonderful

follower of Christ I had ever witnessed. She was

also becoming a young woman with great

passion for sharing her love for The Lord in a

manner I never imagined. Together we searched

for the answers she was so desperate to find and

both of us had grown deeper in our faith.

Christy, however, was immersed in His love so

much that it was evident in her face whenever

she began talking to anyone. Her ability to talk

about Christ was always unique, and she shared

her faith whenever the opportunity arose. My

heart would flutter every time I saw her or heard

of the things she was doing. My little girl with

the self esteem issue was now a young lady who

was never afraid to share her love for Jesus. Her

heart seemed to explode with love and

compassion for others, and she was on fire.

Christy was not only growing in her faith, but also was physically getting taller everyday. We were buying new shoes for her every two weeks, and she quickly grew taller than her brother by just an inch. How was it that my daughter was seven inches taller than me? I would remain the shortest member of our family at just under five feet tall. Because Christy never wanted to ask for anything, she would often not say anything about her clothes not fitting, and would most often wear her shoes as long as she could until it was no longer comfortable.

When Christy arrived as a seventh grader in middle school, the English teacher identified a group of students on her team that had an ability to write. She formed a portfolio group and had this handful of students write a variety of things such as poetry, short stories, essays, and more. The group began writing a newsletter that was published weekly and printed for the students. Essays that these students wrote were submitted to various contests. Christy was part of this select group when she was in seventh grade and she thrived in it. She wrote so many different pieces they soon filled up a very large binder. Her eighth grade English teacher continued working with Christy, and by the time she finished middle school, she had won several writing contests and was awarded scholarship money. She was presented with awards in front of her peers during the school day. One of the essays that she wrote in seventh grade was submitted for a contest but did not win. However, it was selected by to be published the following year in a children's literacy publication. *Kaleidoscope Magazine*—through The Michigan Reading Association—chose her piece, and we traveled three hours for her to be honored with other students at a reception. We were so proud of her.

For inspiration to write this particular piece, Christy's teacher had given her a stack of various magazines to look through. I remember sitting with her thumbing through the pages of these periodicals. As we sat chatting, Christy stumbled upon a picture in a copy of *Life Magazine*. It was from 1997 with a picture of Oprah on the front. A very short article tucked away on the side of the left page explained the picture she had found of a little baby boy wrapped up tightly in a blanket with an empty bottle next to him. He was lying there in the midst of a forest, abandoned. The story was of American travelers that stumbled upon this child and took him to the hospital. This led Christy to think deeper about what we now refer to as the One-Child Policy in China.

The One-Child policy began around 1980 when the Chinese government decided to regulate the population size by enforcing a strict policy that each family was only allowed to have one child. While the policy is no longer officially in place, the ideology that it ingrained in the people of China still shows that it is in many ways still practiced. Some of the negative effects such as a preference of male children and abandoning a girl child or an unhealthy baby still occur today.

After learning about the one-child policy herself, Christy wrote this piece entitled, "What

I Would Do Now to Make My World a Better
Place".

What I Would Do Now To Make My World A

Better Place

By

Christy DePriest

Hoover Middle School

Taylor, Michigan

I would begin making my world a better

place now by informing people in and around

my community of how young lives in China are

being destroyed. I would begin this mission first

by telling members of my church to pray,

writing editorials in local and school

newspapers, and sharing this story with as

many people as my voice is able to reach.

Christ with a y

After reading an article one day, I had a sadness in my heart that will not leave my mind. Lying in the middle of the two pages of a magazine I was browsing through was a baby boy. He was left alongside a path just off a small road in the very populated country of China. The child was discovered by a group of Americans who took him to a hospital. The staff was puzzled and a little amused at the concern of the Americans. The boy was suffering from pneumonia and a deformed heart. Returning to the same location, the Americans discovered another baby that died one day later.

How many other babies have been left abandoned to die a slow, lonely death? In this country the population continues to increase by 13 million children born yearly. The government has issued a law to only allow couples 1 to 2 children. This law is known to the Chinese as the One Couple, One Child Policy. This is to keep the population from increasing to reduce the risk of famine.

It is also a custom in China that the boys are responsible for their aging parents. There is no form of social security available to the people that can no longer work. If a girl is born or a baby with birth defects (as in the case of the baby found by the road), the child may be abandoned and left to die in hopes of being able to later bare a son.

Another pitiful element in this saga is how babies are aborted even at a late stage in pregnancies for the reasons of disobeying the One Couple, One Child Policy. Birth control is strongly advised but is not always an effective method.

Christ with a Y

*How painful for the parents of these babies
to live the rest of their lives in guilt knowing
they had to destroy a precious life because of a
law. How fortunate we are in the United States
not to have to live in such a way. It is God's
plan as to how our families are to be made up.
Morally and ethically, people should not be
making these decisions.*

*I would like to make my world a better
place now by letting these people know that it
would not be a disgrace to let people from other
countries adopt these fragile, little lives. It has
been successfully done in many countries.
Maybe if I am able to make others aware of this
crisis and we pray about it, we can make a
difference.*

*It is my dream that through our prayers
and our voices, we will be heard and can make*

a difference to change such a heart wrenching situation. Because I have been loved unconditionally, I will strive to accomplish this mission. Let us give the Chinese a choice...not a policy.

We had no idea at the time Christy wrote this piece that it would be the beginning of something that would change our lives in the future.

~Chapter Six~

Christy became an entirely new person

during her two years at Hoover Middle School.

My relationship with her changed into

something I had hoped would happen. She was

growing into a young woman who was fun,

curious, and so serious about how she wanted

her life to be. Most days were filled with staying

after school for a sport or going to a music

lesson. After the events of the school day,

Christy could be found in her bedroom playing
her flute, doing homework, reading a book, and
ending the night with her Bible. I would often
spend time with her at the side of her bed
talking about her day. This is something my
mom did with me as a teen-aged girl most every
night. It was special to me to have a mom who
invested her time and love in me. These were
the moments I wanted to share with my
daughter as well.

I didn't grow up with my parents telling
me they loved me every single day. They didn't
have to, because they showed love to me all the
time. I know I told my kids I loved them more
often as they were growing up. I think it was
just a parenting style during my childhood and I
never thought anything about it. To this day, I

would much rather be shown love than to have the words recited out of habit.

Christy studied constantly in order to get the grades she wanted. Her writing was continually getting better during seventh and eighth grade. Many of her essays and stories were entered into contests by her teachers. There were scholarships available through these contests which Christy won several. It was a nice amount of money to put away for college. She had written papers on the importance of The Detroit River, how she would make the world a better place, and others. She received certificates along with checks or sometimes savings bonds during a special assembly during the school day. I would always get an invitation to attend and made sure to go. It was always a proud mom moment!

There were many people who influenced Christy during middle school which made a difference in her life. Her character developed into more than I could have hoped for. Watching her begin to have so much confidence yet still filled with humility put a smile on my face. I was very proud of my daughter because there was more to her than others probably saw. As her mom, I could tell she had a determination that was different from anyone I had known.

Christy had grown tall quickly during these two years. We assumed she would be short like me. I never quite reached the five foot mark and Christy had passed me up by seven inches. Josh was barely keeping up in height with her which made him mad. I never thought it was possible for our daughter to be so tall.

She thought it was great to be taller than her mom and teased me all the time. Ben was taller than me by the time he left elementary school.

Swimming, basketball, track, and cheerleading were the sports Christy participated in as a middle schooler. She had a box filled with ribbons and awards she had gotten from the events she did, plus a shelf full of trophies. She wasn't exceptional at basketball and track, but she was quite the swimmer doing well in backstroke. There were times when all three kids were playing a sport at the same time. Jeff and I would have to juggle our schedules to make sure we were at each of their activities. Going from an outdoor track meet to watch one child run in the chilly spring to a humid natatorium to watch another swim was tiring. We would then drive over to the baseball fields to watch the third child play catcher in a little league game. We were just grateful we could work things out to support each of them in their sport.

Joshua and Christy had not been in the same school building for four years, but that was all about to change. They would be reunited in high school as a junior and a freshman at Harry S Truman High School.

Christy was signed up for Marching Band which meant a week at band camp. Josh had already experienced this as a trumpet player a few years earlier. I had been involved with band as a coach for the Pom and Flag Team so I was able to be part of camp. It was a very rigorous time for the group, especially for the freshman. Christy was excited to attend though and she did well. Many of the members were friends with Josh and they recognized Christy as his little sister. The girls took Christy under their wing and made her feel comfortable.

Band camp was on a lake about ninety minutes from our home. They worked hard during the day on the halftime show they would perform during home football games during the fall. They would do fun things at night and get to know each other better. There were some occasional shenanigans that took place which made for a lot of great memories. Taking down scaffolding from outside and putting it back together inside the cafeteria was one of the best stories I had heard.

It was fun watching Christy prepare for high school through band camp. It gave her an opportunity to feel more comfortable before her first day of classes. I loved how Josh's friends were making her feel good about the days ahead

that are usually frightening for freshman

students.

~Chapter Seven~

The day had arrived in late August for

Christy to start her first day of high school. We

had gone clothes shopping because it was

always what we did at the end of summer before

school began. The irony of this was it was still

summer and most days were quite warm and

sometimes downright hot with temperatures in

the low nineties. The new clothes would

generally not get worn until the beginning of
October.

We lived close enough to the school that
our kids could walk and there were no buses for
our neighborhood. Josh was already driving and
had his own car. It was a Pontiac Grand Prix
that was sporty. It was a turquoise color with a
small backseat. Christy's backpack took up as
much space in that backseat as a small child.
Josh was not happy taking his sister to school
complaining her things just didn't fit. He
blamed her for anything that was broken trying
to figure out a way to change this situation. We
told him he had to drive her because it just made
sense. He just didn't want his sister with him
and it made her sad that he felt that way. It was
just one of those sibling issues they had with
each other.

Christ with a Y

As the Class of 2003 walked the halls, the upperclassmen began to take notice of the young ladies. Josh was annoyed with this as his friends were among those gentlemen talking to his sister. She was asked to The Homecoming Dance by one of his good friends and he was a little bothered. We could see a little change of heart now in Josh for his sister. Although he wasn't happy about her going to a dance with his friend, he still didn't like driving her to school. It was a cool thing to see that he truly cared about Christy.

Shopping for Christy's first dance was really fun. She found a long black gown that fit her perfectly. She had her hair done up, put on the dress with a pair of black heels before her date arrived with a wrist corsage. It was hard to believe how grown up Christy looked and how well she carried herself that night. She was

given a curfew by her dad and a stern look was

passed off to the young man as he reiterated the

time he was to have her home.

As the middle of the school year

approached, Christy was noticed by a young

man who was a senior. We were concerned over

their age difference. We felt with strong

supervision, it would be alright for them to date.

He was a wonderful young man from a great

family. The biggest obstacle in this dating

relationship was the difference in their faith.

Each of them was deeply rooted in their beliefs

with neither of them willing to budge. It caused

great stress on their relationship which

fascinated me. It wasn't that they weren't both

Christians and that they didn't believe in

salvation through Jesus. It was just some of their

views on other ways they believed. Knowing how strong Christy was and how she would not waiver was simply amazing to observe from my perspective.

The two decided it would be better to be friends than continue in a relationship that would be divided by their differences. I'm quite sure that this was Christy's first love as I saw the heartbreak she suffered for a few weeks. She was so young, but she already exhibited an ability to know what was good for her. She trusted in what God wanted for her. Christy sought His plan for her rather than trusting in herself and what the world thought. She was simply incredible to watch as she just kept growing stronger in her faith and keeping Christ centered in her life.

Christy was still pouring all her energy into everything she was involved in at this point. She was keeping her grades up only suffering through difficult math classes while staying involved in so many extracurricular activities. She was exhausted every night after her long days, but kept every commitment she made.

Christy was babysitting children, working at our local recreation department, and then getting a part-time job in retail. After getting her purse stolen out of her locker one day at this job, her dad wanted her to leave that position. She and her friend, Traci, decided to stop in at the new Texas Roadhouse restaurant that had recently opened to apply for a hostess position. One of my favorite stories about Christy and her dad was when she came home from applying for this job. He had told our kids to never apply for a position with a friend. This, of course, only motivated Christy to see if she could prove him wrong—something she thoroughly enjoyed doing to her dad. As no surprise to me, Traci and Christy were both hired on the spot.

Not only did the girls get interviewed together, they both let the establishment know they were unavailable to work on Sunday or Wednesday because they both went to church on those days. They stood firm on that statement as their priorities were to first serve the Lord. Watching her dad's jaw drop to the floor when Christy told him this was absolutely priceless. All he could do was smile and shake his head at his strong-willed daughter. This was just the first of many times Christy would take on a challenge with her dad and prove him wrong.

Her relationship with him was pretty special and I loved watching them work things out during disagreements.

Christy, like Josh, only lasted a little while in the band program. It was very time consuming and since she was involved in so many other things, thought it would be better to put her time into those things. She continued with her flute lessons and began playing in the newly formed church orchestra and for special music during services. I was so happy to be able to accompany her on the piano for some of these specials. She had me do this for her while she was going to band competitions as well.

No matter what Christy took on, she would give it everything she had, which made things she did look easy to others. Whatever she did, she did it for the Lord. She had a natural

ability to show those around her the love she
had for Jesus. It was beautiful authentic and
sincere. This is something I will repeat over and
over again about my daughter, because my heart
overflowed with humility that the Lord would
bless me with a child like Christy.

High school had its ups and downs for
Christy. There were many days that she felt
defeated by her peers. She was unique and she
struggled with that because many people didn't
understand her motivation for telling others
about Jesus. High school is a tough crowd
because everyone is figuring out life and how to
be accepted. Christy couldn't figure out why
people weren't easily accepting her words and
desire for them to come to church with her. She
didn't let the world persuade her which was an
extraordinary characteristic trait I adored in her.

There were many dances Christy attended with a new dress in a different color each time. She had so many funny stories about her dates—some that weren't so good which brought out a side of her that was pretty interesting. She would not be disrespected by anyone.

In the fall of 2002, Christy was voted onto the six member Homecoming Court. The tradition was to wear a large hooped gown to the assembly on Friday morning for the announcement of who would be queen. Christy found a gorgeous violet dress that fit her as if it had been made for her. She accessorized it with above the elbow satin gloves with a pearl necklace and matching earrings. Each girl was given a tiara with rhinestones and a white sash to wear.

Christ with a y

The girls were excused from school the day of the big event so they could get all dolled up. Christy had her hair put up with curls falling from the crown of her head. The tiara was placed perfectly on the top of her head and she looked amazing. Once again, my girl looked even more grown up than she had at any other time. She was beautiful and I couldn't stop smiling. Each of the girls did the same that morning getting all dressed up in different color dresses. Yellow, white, red, blue, and gold were the other hues selected by the young ladies.

The assembly began with each girl being separately escorted by a young man who was selected as a court member to be crowned Homecoming King. The lights were dimmed in the beautifully decorated gymnasium. It was filled with arches of balloons and white runways. The entered the back of the room with their favorite song playing walking up to a stage where six wicker chairs awaited them. Christy entered to the song "A Moment like This" by Kelly Clarkson. It was one of her first songs and Christy thought the title was fitting for her. She was so honored to be part of this day.

Christy was not crowned queen that day, but she was happy for her friend that did. She really didn't put much emphasis on being queen because she was just ecstatic to be part of the court. She was given bouquets of flowers that filled her arms. Christy was a happy girl and I was so happy for her.

A parade was scheduled for early evening followed by the football game. Each class had built a float that was themed. From late summer until this day in late October the classes worked hard on their creations, which were built on trailer beds. Chicken wire held flowers made from colored trash bags and made into some incredible displays. The route of the parade was down a side street to the main road where the high school was located spanning about a mile. The floats, the marching band, cheerleaders, and court were among the participants in the line up.

When we found out Christy was on court, we needed to find a convertible car for her and her escort to ride in for the parade. We couldn't find one to borrow or rent so we had a bit of fun with this adventure. We shopped for a vehicle to purchase. This was the last year Chevrolet was going to make the Camaro and Jeff always had a thing for this car. After searching for a few days, we found a brand new

2002 black convertible with a V8 engine, black leather seats and an automatic transmission. Normally an awesome car like this should be a standard shift, however, I had never learned how to drive like that and Jeff knew that if he wanted to do this for his little girl, he'd have to compromise. We purchased the car and drove it home in a downpour of rain laughing at what we had just done. We rarely did anything that spontaneous so it made it really special for us.

Jeff washed and waxed the car to prepare it for the parade. He put a big blanket on the top of the back seat so she would be comfortable and not scratch anything. Christy looked so pretty in her violet dress that took up the entire back seat. Her dad was proudly driving her through the streets while she sat there waving to people lining the street. Her escort was dressed in a black tuxedo next to her making their way to the football field behind the school.

When the football players finished the first two quarters of the game, the halftime show began. The band performed their show, the floats made their way around the track, and the court was announced and introduced. The winner of the float was the Senior Class and the girls made their way around the track in golf carts. It was a night that Christy would not forget because it was all about her and her friends celebrating their last year of high school.

The following evening was the dance that was held inside the school gymnasium. Jeff and I volunteered as chaperones having a great time watching our daughter have an amazing evening. Our second child would soon be making her way into the adult world and it had gone by so quickly. We were beginning to ponder on the thoughts of where Christ's life would go. Where would God plant her and use her? Would He introduce her to a man who would become her groom she was now praying for soon? So many questions were popping into my mind because I knew the next few years would fly by for Christy.

As winter began to approach during that year, Christy would start to realize who and what were important to her. Friendships began to shift, and the focus on what was really important began to be revealed. Christy decided to end her cheerleading days and focus on planning the prom that would be coming up. She was class president, so it was up to her and the rest of the class officers' job to plan the event. Christy was well organized, good at planning, so she placed her focus on this project. She chose the venue and arranged all the things she needed to do to make their prom a night to remember.

I told Christy that we would not purchase another large hooped gown for this event, explaining that we had many expenses coming up with graduation and our second child who would be in college. Jeff and I were never about our kids having everything and wanted them to be responsible adults. We continually made sure they had what they needed with some extras thrown in, but also made it obvious that they would one day be independent young people. They were given a vehicle to drive, but fuel, insurance, and minor repairs were their responsibility. They were given brand new clothes at the beginning of the school year, but anything they wanted in addition was up to them.

Christy wished to wear a blue gown as this was the color that dazzled her eyes when she dressed in every shade of this hue. She saved her money over the next several months, so she could purchase the most divine dress. When it arrived, it fit her as if it had been specifically designed for her just like the violet dress from Homecoming did. This dress was strapless with a bodice filled with elegant designs. The skirt was embroidered with pretty accents with a big bow in the back at her waist. She tucked it away in her closet as she awaited the event.

It was a busy, busy year for Christy, planning for so many things, keeping up with homework, and working. She was continuously

exhausted, but never let anything go. She would

nap whenever she had a minute, even if the nap

only lasted a few moments, and I noticed this

was more than just ordinary tiredness. Christy's

throat was hurting more than it should have

been and she was filled with nausea almost

every morning. Headaches, that would put her

in tears, were common on a daily basis, so we

began visiting the family doctor. He ordered

blood work to rule out things like mono, and

everything would come back within the normal

range. Medication was given to Christy for the

headaches, and he ordered a CT scan for further

testing. That, too, was negative for any issues.

We were taking her to the doctor's office quite

frequently during this year with no results. It

was decided to take her to be tested for allergies,

and once we found out how many things she was sensitive to, she began weekly injections. They seemed to help with some of her symptoms, but she just began to tolerate her conditions. These issues were not severe enough to take further action on, but it seemed as if Christy was just not the healthiest version of herself. Her friends were just as active as she was, but were not having the same difficulties with exhaustion. It sometimes bothered me that she wanted to sleep whenever she could, and it was hard for me to understand.

Although we were making recurrent visits to the doctor, Christy continued to manage her daily routine. She was becoming more and more confident and independent. I sat back and gazed at this child often. I was amazed at how she dealt with life and all it threw at her. I marveled at her inner strength and compared it to mine. She was so much more at this age than I was. I let myself get wrapped up in the world more than I wish I would have, looking more for the acceptance of my friends rather than focusing on the acceptance of God. Christy was nothing like that; she sought Jesus every single day. I know she was ridiculed for this but she stood firm and kept herself from falling into the ways of the world. Was she perfect? Absolutely not. Some days were much harder than others for her to get up in the morning and face criticism, but she counted on the mercy of God that is made new each day.

Being a mom is a tough task as we must sit back and watch our child's hearts get broken, but as we know, this is how they are molded into adults. I have always tried to be the parent first but also their friend, as I always wanted them to be able to come to me and tell me whatever they needed to talk about. I planted myself in their lives and tried to teach them how to put God first, and the conversations I have had with each of my kids has been humbling for me.

I remember telling Christy to hold on tight to her values and how many would try to tear her down. It was an accurate statement as it happened more times than not. I also told her that one day people would ask her how she managed to stay true to her ways. Before the middle of her senior year she began getting that question asked. It made me smile when she came to me to tell me that what I had told her a few years ago was happening.

Christ with a Y

While working at Texas Roadhouse,
Christy had met a young lady with long blonde
hair named Kimmie. This girl did not really care
too much for Christy at first. She had overheard
Christy talking one day about where she hoped
to attend college. Kimmie began talking to her
as she had a similar interest in this cool. This
sparked a friendship that was like no other I had
ever seen. These two girls would become the
best of friends and share many memories
together.

Jeff and I took them down to Liberty
University in Lynchburg, Virginia for a
weekend visit, and while there, they tried out for
the sports teams they each loved. Christy's
desire was to be on the cheerleading squad and
Kimmie's the softball team. They gave their
best effort, but neither was chosen, and that was

just fine with them. They were both strong women knowing they would be better suited somewhere else on the campus. After just one weekend, both girls knew this was the place they wanted to attend college without a doubt. It was an amazing experience for me to watch my daughter getting ready to begin her life away from home. Some people would have felt great anxiety to know their daughter would be so far away from home, but I was excited for Christy. I was thrilled to see her doing things I had not experienced, and knowing she was following God's plan for her life. Christy belonged at this school, and I could see her face glowing no matter where we went that weekend. It was all she talked about for weeks after we arrived back home. The realization she would really be going away started to settle in. I was a bit stirred when

I thought about not having the daily face to face interactions with her. I looked forward to hearing about her daily escapades as they captured my attention regularly. She had such an extraordinary style of dealing with the ways of the world. Christy was a breath of fresh air everyday for me. Even on the days her peers or life in general knocked her back, she faced every new day with tenacity.

The end of the school year had come and it was time for prom. The guys and girls were running for prom queen and king now. Christy had decided not to put her name in because she thought it was only fair for others to be part of this since she had already experienced being on homecoming court. Her name was written in by her peers anyway, and she was voted queen. What a great honor to be recognized for her hard work! Jeff and I were so happy for her, but she remained extremely humbled and felt she did not deserve this. That was Christy everyday, all the time.

Christy's car was not very reliable for long trips so we needed her to have something that would do well while she was traveling back and forth from Virginia. Because of her accomplishments and scholarship money, we decided it was best to purchase a new car for her. We took her to the dealer and she chose a blue Saturn Ion. It was fitting for her as this girl loved all things blue. She finished her last few weeks of high school driving this new car.

Graduation day finally arrived and it was filled with so many different emotions. The joy of my daughter finishing her four years of high school was the best feeling. The realization that she was quickly becoming an adult and would

soon be off to college made me heart a little sad.

A bit of pride swelled within me to think about

all she had accomplished to this point in her life.

Just a bit of relief to know Christy had survived

the pressures of being high school teenager

made me smile.

Christy, being class president, gave a

speech to the graduates. We spent hours

working on it together, and she presented it at

the farewell graduation assembly a few days

before the formal ceremony. It was also her

privilege to dismiss each row of graduates as

they received their diplomas.

Christy graduated with honors and we

were so very proud of all she had accomplished

while in high school. She made the best of each

day, and we knew she would do well while in

college. We held a big party for her in our backyard with family and friends to celebrate her achievements. It was a warm, humid day with a few rain showers to send guests running under the tents we rented. With the open house party, people were filing in and out of our backyard at their leisure. By the time the festivities of the day had ceased, Christy was ready for some rest. It was a big day filled with joy and happiness!

We had been planning for college life while finishing up all the activities of high school with Christy. Paperwork for classes and finding the right dorm became a top priority throughout that time. The biggest concern of all for Kimmie and Christy though was who the third roommate would be. Of all the things to be concerned over, this was the biggest. The

Christ with a Y

summer months following Christy's graduation
were filled with going back and forth online
searching for a dorm room with three openings.
It took the entire summer for everything to work
out, and gratefully, it did. They would have to
wait until August to meet the "mysterious"
roommate.

~Chapter Eight~

The summer of 2003 passed by so

quickly, and the day had finally arrived to pack

up our truck and the blue Saturn Ion to head for

Lynchburg, Virginia. Kimmie followed along in

our "mini caravan" which traveled south, where

college life began five hundred miles away. The

university campus was the most beautiful place

I had ever visited. Not only because of its

location hidden in a valley amidst The Blue

Ridge Mountains, but because of the story of

how it began. It's a place where the saying

"Training Champions for Christ" is taken

seriously and the presence of God surrounds

you everywhere.

Christy and Kimmie were exuberant the

morning we left. It was a hot summer day in

mid-August and it began to rain upon our arrival

to campus. This first day on campus, the rain

could not dampen the girl's spirits. Today was

the day they met the third girl, who would round

out their three-woman dorm room and they were

thrilled when they met her. Amanda was a

sweet, quiet girl with long blonde hair. She was

a perfect fit and all was wonderful in the world

of girls. All the worry and curiosity over the

summer was now washed away. All three girls

were getting to know each other quickly as they figured out their living arrangements. The room was on the third floor of the dorm and contained two closets, a set of twin size bunk beds, a single twin bed, and three small desks. All three families were there helping get the room set up, and the girls had fun meeting all the new faces on their floor. Even amid all the fun the girls were having, it was a stressful time. Having been to Lynchburg once before, we didn't know our way around well enough, which meant that inevitable trips for miscellaneous items needed took on more of a journey feel than a quick hop to the store. It was a fun but stressful time as none of us were familiar with the area or the things we had to get taken care of in the short time we would be there.

Christ with a Y

Christy fit right into this dynamic, which

steadied my resolve about how my little girl

would handle this change of scenery. Christy's

little brother, Ben, had accompanied us on this

trip to assist in any way he could. He was good

with construction and computers. He wanted to

see where his sister would be spending the next

four years, as well as spend time with her before

saying farewell. We left Christy Sunday

evening with her new friends. Saying, "See you

soon", to her was not an easy task, but I held

back my tears as I watched my eighteen-year-

old daughter walk away with her head hanging.

Her backpack was strapped to her back, and she

was headed into a whole new life with love and

support from us. Jeff and Ben struggled, and

tears were falling from their eyes as we pulled

away. No one could speak. In my heart I knew

Christy would experience things I had never been through.

Living away from home in a totally different state unable to be around people she knew well and learning how to be somewhat independent at eighteen years old. Christy would be driving around a new town all by herself without seeking parental permission. I lived with my parents until I was married never leaving the city I was raised in. My independence was gained in a much different way than Christy's was. She would be homesick, but learn how to live an independent life which I admired. She would also learn more about Jesus and what His plans for her were. She would find new friends, gain knowledge, and become a responsible adult. She would become a leader and a prayer warrior, as well as a professional in a field of her chosen course of study. I smiled and my heart was ready to explode watching Christy walk away from what was familiar and comfortable—her family. She was now on her way into a God-centered future. Christy was right where He wanted her and that gave me the greatest calm. I was reminded of a bible verse to give all my worrying to Christ. Peter writes in First Peter, "Cast all your anxiety on Him because He cares for you." I knew He cared for Christy.

Christy carried more than a full load of credit hours in college, and worked more than part time at Texas Roadhouse as a server. Of course, she was also involved in ministries such as being a Prayer Leader on her floor and later a Student Life Director. She loved working with her friends and helping them see the wonderful things God could do in their lives. Her words were simple and beautiful when she shared her relationship with Christ. Her role as a Student Life Director was to counsel the girls and help them with accountability, which she was always passionate about. Christy was completely and fully engaged as this was her ultimate comfort zone.

Whenever Christy would call and talk to her dad and brothers, they were happy, but Jeff often shed a little tear as he missed his girl. I later found this sweet little note he had written and mailed to her:

> *I am very proud of you.*
> *Remember why you are at*
> *school. Try your best and have*
> *fun doing it. These could be some*
> *of the best days of your life.*

Don't sweat the small stuff. Keep
your priorities in line. It will be
very important to manage your
time. Try to work enough to have
spending money but not so much
to affect your studies. Be careful
who you trust. Remember all men
have come short of the glory of
God. Even good people can do
bad things. We are several
hundred miles away but only a
day drive or a couple of hours
plane ride. If you really need us,
we will be there. Don't forget to
call to let us know how things are
or if you need something. I love
you and see you soon.

~Dad

Christy's first visit home was in October

when the school gave everyone some time to be

with family as homesickness began to set in for

all. I think Christy was a little homesick, but

after the time home, she knew how much fun she was having at Liberty. Off she and Kimmie went driving down the road to their new temporary place in Virginia. It was so encouraging to see the maturity level of these girls as they pulled away honking their horn and blaring their music. Again, my tears were not present, only a big smile—I couldn't say the same for Jeff! Every time she pulled away he would be a little sad.

Christy traveled home for all holidays, which was nice. One of her trips home to Michigan was rather difficult because she was extremely ill. She drove the entire five hundred miles and went to the doctor as soon as she arrived. Her symptoms were flu-like, and the entire Christmas break was spent trying to get her better. I cried Christmas Eve when she was unable to get out of bed to celebrate with our family. I could not believe how sick my poor girl was and how nothing we tried was helping her feel better. It seemed that this "flu" had literally taken her out. Thankfully, the Christmas break was lengthy and she had time to recuperate. With a lot of rest she was able to return to school in mid-January and seemed to be alright. It was as though the same symptoms she was dealing with in high school all came together and hit her hard. I never completely concluded that she had the flu but something more serious. However, after it subsided, I dismissed it.

The first two years living in a dorm were great, but Kimmie and Christy had a desire to live off campus in an apartment. At the end of their sophomore year they began the search, and on one of our visits we went around town

looking with them for a safe place to live. We

were not real thrilled with this idea, but the girls

wanted to gain more independence and insisted

they would pay for their own rent and groceries.

The only thing we took care of was tuition.

They found a cute place not far off campus and

moved into a second floor apartment with one

bedroom, one bathroom, a kitchen, and living

room. The bedroom was large and

accommodated their furniture but also gave

them separate spaces. Both parents brought

gently used furniture from home for them and

they had a quaint place to call home. Of course,

the patterns were a little chaotic with each piece

being from different eras. The brown and rust

floral patterned chair met up with a blue striped

recliner. The black dorm chair and the gold

sleeper sofa clashed with the beige shag carpet.
It made no difference to the girls because the
only thing they cared about was their new found
independence. Only one month after moving in,
the roof began to leak and they were moved to
another apartment. All that work setting up their
new home only to move and start again.
Fortunately, the girls were resourceful and
found some college guys to help them move all
their furniture.

Christy met many new friends at
Liberty, one of her closest was a girl named
Susan. They took a weekend trip to Chicago in
March to attend a Women's Conference at a
university, so Jeff and I decided to drive over to
spend a few hours with Christy and her friend.
We did a lot of walking and talking that day,
and it was so worth the trip to see our girl. It

was an enjoyable day for us shopping and eating great food while checking out the Windy City. Whenever the opportunity arose for us to be with Christy we took it, and I will forever be grateful that we took those occasions to make memories.

Susan continued to play an important role in Christy's life, and a solid friendship was formed between them. The friendships that Christy had with people were never casual. She was the type of person to be true to everyone. Kimmie and Susan were women she trusted and loved because they held the same beliefs as she did. They could agree to disagree, but more times than not they helped to carry each other through various circumstances that arose. It is a beautiful thing to have friends that have great faith and will stand alongside of one another through the storms of life. But, good friends also are needed to help celebrate the blessings each other receives in life. Close friendships are rare and should never be taken for granted. These girls took this to heart and were the closest of friends.

~Chapter Nine~

The summer of 2005 was a very interesting, busy, and crazy season. While we were in Lynchburg helping Kimmie and Christy search for an apartment, Christy came to us and began asking our thoughts on her taking a missions trip to Africa. This bombshell caught both of us off guard, and we had a difficult time thinking about our daughter traveling so far away with a group of people we did not know.

But we promised her we'd think about it and continue to pray for guidance. Eventually, the trip was canceled. We weren't out of the woods yet, however. Around this same time Christy was approached about another mission's opportunity: a trip to China. If the thought of Africa was a gut-punch, the idea of Christy traveling to China was a complete blindsided punch. The decision wasn't easy, there was simply too much to think about, but there was also history with this country and our family— the essay Christy wrote in middle school.

This essay became important in the decision making process. How was it that the words she had written were becoming part of a story of her life?

Jeff continued to tell Christy he did not feel comfortable with her going to China, but she was persistent with her intentions. While home during a break from school, Christy told her dad that she was going to spend an hour and a half in her room explaining why she felt she should be able to take this trip with his consent. She said that after her explanation, if he again said no, she would never bring it up again and would not go. Christy had such a way of presenting herself, and once she came out of her room and gave her reasons to Jeff, he told her she could go. The tears in his eyes after her speech said it all. He knew he couldn't go against what God was calling Christy to do. He knew he could not interfere with His calling in her life and His plan for her. This was not something we were surprised about when Christy's desires became obvious for the mission field, but it was hard for us to let our daughter travel to such a far away place. She was doing this alone without knowing anyone traveling with her.

There were so many things to do to prepare for this trip. She wrote letters to friends, family, and church members for support. All the money was raised for the trip, but there were many other expenses. Christy needed a passport, as well as, many shots to make sure she was protected from diseases. We had quite a time finding where she could get these injections, but managed to get everything necessary and recommended. As she began taking the malaria medication, it made her nauseated, but she continued to take it weeks before the trip to ensure she would not contract anything.

As Christy was preparing for this big trip, my dad had been building a house next door to his. It was a beautiful home that I tried not to fall in love with because I knew with two college students we could not possibly afford. One day my very financial savvy husband announced to me that he was thinking about the house and how we might be able to purchase it. It was time filled with big decisions and stress, albeit wonderful yet frightening. We put our house up for sale where our family began and it sold quickly. In mid-May we began to move our things slowly to the new house. We had to run down to Virginia to bring Christy home for the summer in the midst of this move, but it just made life more fun and interesting. We brought her back with many of her things, and she spent only a few nights in our old house before we moved everything over.

Jeff had a business trip scheduled just a couple of weeks after our move and was able to take me with him. We had a death in the family as we were ready to leave, so we couldn't stay home to attend the funeral. Christy and Ben were left home. She helped Ben get dressed and took him to the funeral. Ben was growing quickly now and his dress clothes were a bit snug, but Christy made sure he looked appropriate for the funeral. After we arrived in Calgary, Alberta, Canada, we called them to see how things went, and all we got was pure laughter out of the conversation. They laughed about Ben's pants that were too short and barely buttoned and how tight his shoes were. "He was lucky his shirt buttoned," Christy said. They never ceased to make us laugh whenever they were together. They just shared the same funny

bone, and it was fun to watch them.

Not long after we returned from this trip,

it was time for Christy to leave for her trip to

Guangzhou, China. She was extremely anxious

about the trip, but at the same time immensely

excited about what she would do there. This was

Christy's first international trip, and since we

couldn't go to the airport with her to see her off,

we found a different plan. Our friend, Pastor

John Reilly, had a security clearance into the

airport, so he kindly took Christy to the airport

and stayed with her until she boarded her flight.

We were so grateful to him for this, and it eased

Christy's anxiety. He picked her up from our

home, and I saw Christy's relief once she

planted herself in the passenger seat of his car.

She knew she would be protected by God and

that her friend and pastor would ease her anxiety through conversation.

Christy flew to Los Angeles, California, where she had a lengthy layover. She called me in tears upon her arrival because she couldn't find her way to the terminal where her next flight would leave, which was the long flight over the Pacific Ocean to China. I felt so bad for her with the inability to help her. I stayed on the phone with her as she continued to walk through LAX looking for where she belonged. After several minutes, she found the group she was meeting up with to continue to China—a relief for both of us! The team got together and decided to leave the airport for a little while, finding their way to the beach. This was so good for Christy to relieve the butterflies she had inside her. Before boarding the plane, once back at the airport, she called me to let me know she was fine and would contact me from China when she could. It was so hard not talking to her for that length of time because we talked every day. Knowing I could not only talk to her but also that I couldn't get to her quickly if she needed me was uncomfortable, but I trusted the Lord to keep her safe. I also trusted that He would keep her dad and I comforted while she was away.

I knew I was placing all my faith in God with this trip because I didn't really even know the group she was traveling with. The trip was an organization that would be teaching English to children during the summer. These were children of families who wished to send their kids to a five week course away from home to learn English as their second language.

Christ with a Y

The trip was really to share a message of
Christ to whomever they could reach. A
message that would change lives and was
dangerous for them. The group of college
students had to come up with a way to do this
without suspicion, and they did it by wearing a
necklace that drew interest. It was a wooden
cross attached to a simple piece of leather, and it
did what they had hoped. In China, it is illegal
to approach someone with the gospel, but the
people are allowed to question someone. The
necklaces drew questions from people, and they
were able to share the good news with those
who had never heard it.

The couple that escorted them around
went by the English names of Jack and Elaine.
Christy talked about them continually when she
emailed or called me. They were determined to

tell them the message of Jesus and they
succeeded. Christy would continue to
communicate with Jack and Elaine for a long
time once she returned, and they were
eventually married.

It was so great to hear from Christy
when she contacted us from Internet cafes. I
remember staying glued to my computer and
having my phone on me at all times waiting for
her. She was very tired, and the Malaria
medicine was still bothering her. She was not
having a great time eating the food, but
managed. She had a lot of American cookies she
found at a market and did her best to eat. I
couldn't believe some of the pictures Christy
showed us of the food when she returned. I
think Christy thought differently about what she

was capable of doing after she came home from China.

It was really interesting to hear Christy talk about her time in China. She was so anxious to come home, and within days of being back, she began talking of her plans to return. She had decided, after much prayer, that this is what she felt called to do with her life. I believe that God had led her to this as far back as the time she wrote that essay in middle school. It was interesting to see the story weaving its way together.

Teaching the children to speak English was something Christy was very good at. She became friends with many of the kids, but one little girl in particular. Her name was "Birdie". She was about nine years old and came from a wonderful family. Christy was not on this trip working with orphaned children, but this is where she made the decision to make that her life mission. I believe that once she had seen her ability to talk with people easily, even though there was a language barrier, she was willing to take on the role God was showing her: the role of a girl on the mission field sharing Jesus to everyone that encountered her face. This girl had a heart that was on fire, and it was fascinating to listen to her passion.

Christy took many pictures with Birdie, and I knew she had attached herself to this little girl. When her parents arrived at the end of the session, she cried saying goodbye to Christy. I knew this brought tears to her eyes, well-knowing she would probably never see this child again. She is all grown up by now, and I wonder if she thinks about Christy and the time spent with her learning new words and how to dance.

There was a young man on this trip that Christy took an interest in, but nothing became of it. My daughter had a very strict list of qualities her future husband must have. She was searching carefully for this person, and the gentleman she had met on this trip just didn't fit the bill. She would continue her search for the man that God designed for her and patiently wait on His timing for that.

After arriving in China, the group leader told them they were on their own. A bunch of college students in southeast China alone to figure things out. This didn't sit well with Jeff or me, and we felt so helpless. Being responsible and resourceful college kids, they worked together and did well to organize the remaining time in Southeast Asia. With Christy being tall and fair, she was stared at by the Chinese people. She was once again like a real life Barbie doll. I know it was strange for Christy to be stared at and her hair touched by complete strangers. Being a target for pick-pocketing was also on their radar, as it was happening to a few of them in the group. They were asked to be on TV one day after being interviewed by a reporter. The people in this part of the country seemed to be intrigued with the group. Christy told me that their appearance was unique, and rarely seen by the people living in southern China. This was pretty cool to them, as well as hilarious, to be somewhat of a celebrity in another country.

My daughter learned so many life lessons while in China. She stayed in a dorm

with no screens in the windows, no air
conditioning, showering with a hose taped to the
wall with only cold water, and sleeping on a
bamboo mat. It was hot and very humid during
the time she was there in the middle of summer,
and most of the things she was used to at home
were very different in China.

The day Christy returned home was such
a relief for us. We were not as worried about her
as we thought we would be while she was gone.
Our trust in God to keep her safe and Christy's
ability to trust Him completely with her mission
got us through the five weeks. She was so tired
when she came home, and the first thing she
said was "I'm never going back". After a restful
nap, her tune changed right away. The next day,
Christy was making plans to return and how she
would do it. She had it all planned out as to

how she would make her life overseas, as long as God wanted that to be plan. Jeff and I smiled at each other and knew this would become a reality sooner than later. We knew that Christy's life would be completely dedicated to the work of the Lord, and He seemed to be shaping her heart for the mission field working with little ones. She was so well equipped for this and her heart was still blazing with her desire to serve.

We had a big sign on the front of our garage door that welcomed Christy home. We had only lived in our new house a few short months, so we weren't sure what our neighbors were thinking when they saw this gigantic banner draped across the door. It was always so much fun for me to see the accomplishments of my children. I never thought my daughter would be so bold and brave. She was so focused on her future, and it totally amazed and amused me that

this was the child that God had given us. I love

that I was chosen to be her mother, and that I

was given the opportunity to watch her develop

into a young woman with such great dedication

to the Lord. Christy was a devoted prayer

warrior too. She never did anything without the

guidance of Christ and asking the Holy Spirit to

fill her as each new day began.

~Chapter Ten~

Two weeks after arriving home from China, it was time for Christy to go back to school and start her life off campus with Kimmie. Before leaving school in the spring, after searching the area for a safe and affordable apartment complex, they had signed a rental agreement that began in August. The fall semester of their junior year had arrived and we traveled down to set up their new living quarters. Kimmie's parents went down as well to help move them in. We had such a great time helping them get everything set up.

Within a few short hours of moving boxes and furniture up the stairs, we began unpacking things. An intruder entered through the opened door and everyone stopped what they were doing. At first, we weren't sure what to do so we just waited to see who would make the first move. The cute little kitten went straight to the corner of the living room and left its mark. Kimmie's mom and I looked at each other with a sigh and everyone else in the room just stood there in disgust! Out went the intruder and the door was closed to keep any other visitors from entering the apartment.

They enjoyed being on their own, and did well taking care of each other. The girls always made sure to pay all their bills on time, never once asking for financial help with their new arrangements. They really were responsible young ladies.

Living off campus meant there was no cafeteria to grab food to eat on the run. Their kitchen was used mainly for heating up quick meals or bringing home carry-out food from nearby restaurants. They learned how to prepare food they could keep as leftovers when time permitted them to cook.

The girls were pleased with their new living arrangement at County Green. I remember being happy they lived on the second floor of the complex. It felt a little safer from break-ins to Jeff and me.

About two weeks after the girls were settled in; a rain storm came through

Christ with a Y

Lynchburg. The roof leaked leaving wet carpet and a hole in the ceiling; an inhospitable environment for two young ladies. They contacted management who decided to give them a different apartment. A handful of college friends helped them move across the complex to a dry second story unit. The learning process of growing up and being an adult was happening quickly.

The apartment had one large bedroom which the girls shared. It was bigger than the dorm rooms they lived in on campus giving them plenty of space. Both of their twin beds were on opposite sides and they split the closet with their clothes. A sleeper sofa we had brought down for them was in the living room for guests. It wasn't a very comfortable bed, but it was good for a couple of girls starting out.

The school year went by quickly with occasional trips home to Michigan for holidays and school breaks. The visits were not as long as before since they were paying their own rent. Longer summer visits changed to shorter ones because they both had jobs and bills to pay.

Christy and Kimmie had a successful first year living off campus. Their extracurricular activity involvement changed and friendships did too. During their years while in college, they had both experienced many things good and bad, but it made them into strong, independent women.

Through their time prior to and during their life in the apartment, Christy was watching her best friend fall in love. Christy also began to wonder when her Mr. Right would come along.

Christ with a Y

She had grown up so much in such a short time. She had just traveled halfway around the world, moved into an apartment, was making plans for her future, and possibly losing her best friend to a boy. I know Christy was praying for God to introduce her to the man He had designed for her. Although, only twenty years old, she felt like the day would never come for that special guy. She had dated quite a few gentlemen, but none of them fit her lengthy list of qualifications in a husband. I often found myself in awe of her ability to stay so focused on the things she desired in life. Her trust in God to provide the right man for her never wavered.

God heard Christy's prayers for a man to show up in her life, and during the spring of 2006, Christy was introduced to a young man named Corey Wright through a mutual friend. This gentleman was from the western side of

Michigan, only one hundred fifty-seven miles

away from our home. Corey had decided on a

whim to attend school at Liberty, and drove

down with all he needed in a backpack,

traveling on a motorcycle!

Amy, their mutual friend, thought about

introducing the two of them one day and just

knew they would be perfect for each other.

Amy, who grew up with Corey, had befriended

Christy while at Liberty. She knew them both

well enough to know there could be a

connection. I remember when Christy told me

she was going to go out with Corey. Their first

date was all about getting to know each other,

and I know they talked for hours. One of my

favorite things that Corey told me about their

first date was that he fell in love with Christy

when she began telling him about her family. He said she told him how perfect her family was and how much she loved everyone. It is always wonderful when you're told by your kids that they love you, but when you hear from someone else what was said, it is very humbling. That lives deep in my heart and always will. I'm glad that Christy thought her family was perfect, but I think she embellished on that a bit.

Jeff and I never wanted Christy to drive from Virginia to Michigan alone. She had two friends that were brother and sister that lived near us that she would bring home on break, and we were happy with that arrangement. We would laugh so hard as they pulled out of our driveway in her compact car. Both siblings were very tall, and they would pack the car so tight there was no leg room except for the driver.

Christy would never let anyone drive her car so
she had all the legroom, but she had to
practically eat the steering wheel to make
enough room for bags in the backseat. On top of
all the luggage that had to go back, so did
computer towers and monitors. I could not
believe that car made so many trips with it being
so loaded with all their belongings. It's a
wonder the tires didn't blow out! Every time
that car pulled out of the driveway to head back
to Liberty, Christy would beep the horn until
she was out of sight. Jeff would always have
tears in his eyes as he waved good-bye. I don't
think there was ever a time she left to go back to
Virginia that he didn't have a hard time keeping
back his emotions. I usually kept mine inside; I
was still in awe of this girl of mine. This

courageous, independent girl was growing into a woman right before our eyes.

One of Christy's very good friends was getting married a few months after Christy began dating Corey, and she was going to bring him home for the wedding celebration. It would be the first time we would meet this young man. I was glad Christy had someone to ride home with her, but she began getting cold feet as the time drew near. I began to worry about how she would get home, and thought about either flying down and riding back with her or purchasing a round-trip plane ticket. I still didn't like Christy traveling by car alone over such a long distance. There are too many things I feared might happen even though she had become an adult.

I remember telling her there was no way she was coming home alone, and I simply asked

her what the issue was. Her answer made me
laugh, explaining why she wasn't sure of the
things she was feeling toward Corey. I think she
actually was falling in love.

Although, Christy had grown up with
brothers, the issue of perspiration and back hair
was unfamiliar to her. She discussed this with
Kimmie and her boyfriend, Mike, and they were
able to ease Christy's thoughts on the matter.
Mike explained to Christy that most every male
sweats and back hair is just part of life. I
laughed when I heard this explanation. I was
also grateful the mystery was solved so easily
for Christy. It's funny now to look back on and
I'm so glad Christy's friends were there for her.
It all worked out, and Corey rode home with
Christy for the wedding. That's right, Corey was

in the passenger seat and Christy drove because she never let anyone drive her car.

When we met Corey, we knew this was the man God had designed for Christy. He was extremely kind and respectful. It was obvious he cared for Christy very much, and we could see in their eyes that there was love shared between them both! There was no awkwardness during this first meeting. Josh and Ben seemed to like Corey and he had no problem carrying on great conversations with Jeff and me. I, personally, enjoyed talking with him because he was easy to talk to, fun-loving, and seemed to fit right into the family.

Josh decided to take Corey to meet up with some friends to play basketball. Corey was more of an outdoorsman guy riding four wheelers, Jeeps, and snowmobiles. He enjoyed hunting and camping. Josh enjoyed organized sports that included a ball. When they returned home, there was a lot of poking fun at Corey's basketball skills. He was such a good sport about the whole thing.

At the wedding, he was introduced to so many people that Christy had been friends with for quite some time. Her whole group of friends from church was there, and they welcomed Corey just as they had welcomed Christy when we began going to this church. He fit right in, and by the end of the evening, it seemed as though they had all been friends for a long time.

Kimmie and her boyfriend, Mike, got engaged and planned to get married in January. I believe Christy struggled with this happening. Although she knew that Kimmie and Mike were getting closer to this day, she knew their friendship would change. Kimmie was more than just a best friend to Christy; she was the closest thing to having a sister. Their friendship would still be bonded together closely, but different in many ways.

Corey and Christy continued to date during the summer months and it was obvious that they were enjoying their time together. I was grateful for God's timing with this gentleman coming into Christy's life.

The evening of Kimmie and Mike's wedding was a cold night early in January. Instead of snow, it rained incredibly hard. The bridal party met at Kimmie's parent's house to get ready. As the bride and maid of honor were ready to head to the ceremony, Christy realized she had locked her keys in her car. Her dad and I had already arrived at the chapel when I received a frantic call from Christy. She wanted to know if she could smash her window with a brick in order to get into the car so Kimmie would not be late for her own wedding. I yelled "NO!" and Jeff wondered what was wrong. I told him, and he took off as quickly as he could to run home for the extra key. He drove as quickly as possible, but one of the bridesmaids rescued the girls and brought them to the chapel. Jeff was able to unlock the car, retrieve Christy's purse, and head back within minutes of Kimmie walking down the aisle. It is funny to look back on now, but we were all frantic and worried about these girls. Christy was in tears and felt horrible but Kimmie's dad was the best by telling her it was all right. He told her that God was protecting them from something that could have happened if they had left on time.

Christ with a y

This just added another great Christy and Kimmie story that we love to look back on. I'm so glad she didn't break that window!

Mike and Kimmie moved to Florida a few days after their wedding for Mike to begin his career. The girls had a long distance friendship now that they weren't used to. They called each other and sent texts to stay in touch and keep their friendship going strong. It was just all part of the experience of becoming adults.

Christy returned to Liberty after the break between semesters, without her best friend and roommate. I knew Christy missed her terribly, but she would be just fine. We had several conversations regarding her new situation because this is what we did. We always talked together when we had the chance.

Christy was concerned about how she would be able to afford the rent on her own. She never wanted to ask us for help. We would have given her the extra money needed to cover the expenses she had, but that was not an option for Christy because she valued her independence. She adjusted her spending and was able to stay in her apartment until summer. Corey lived in a small apartment across town so he was around all the time keeping Christy company.

Christy was facing the most difficult class of her undergraduate studies during her last semester: Corporate Finance. It was a class that she needed for her business degree, and although she struggled with it, she would not be easily defeated. She actually befriended the professor along with his wife, and became a caregiver for their children. Christy adored these children, and I heard about them every time we talked on the phone. Christy was always in her element when children surrounded her. She gave them every bit of her attention when she was with them no matter how tired she was.

A full load of classes, babysitting, working, a fiancé, and church activities kept Christy so busy once again. She would even turn down invites to go out in the evening with friends to keep her grades as high as she could. I know of a time she went to a movie with friends and slept because it was the only time she could. She was always there when someone needed a shoulder to cry on or help with school. She was everyone's cheerleader, and flashed her smile even when her heart was sad. It's just what she did. That was Christy.

~Chapter Eleven~

While Christy was busy helping Kimmie plan her wedding, something special took place for her too. In October of 2006, Corey made plans to travel up to our home while Christy was on a little trip to an amusement park in upstate Virginia. We met Corey at Texas Roadhouse and we had a casual conversation while he tried hard to get a cheeseburger down his throat. Jeff and I had a pretty good feeling what was about to go down, but we played it cool. Nothing was mentioned at the restaurant, and when we returned home, I was asked to leave the room for a bit. I was overjoyed when I was asked to leave and that Corey had the respect to ask Jeff for his daughter's hand in marriage. I know that Christy was wondering why Corey came to see us, but I am pretty sure she had an idea why. She kept calling me to find out why he was there, and I kept telling her I just didn't know.

About ten minutes later, I was called back into the living room and was told that Corey had asked Jeff if he could marry our daughter. I was so elated to know we would be gaining a son-in-law. One that we knew was perfect for Christy. We loved Corey and how happy he made Christy.

The next weekend, Corey took Christy
to Crabtree Falls on a hike. It was a park in the
mountains of Virginia they had been to on a few
occasions. It was a beautiful place to hike up to
a waterfall, which Christy loved. He asked her
to marry him on that fall day with leaves all
over the ground and a chill in the air. Of course,
she said yes with a sparkle in her eye. They
traveled back to Michigan the following
weekend to show us the ring and begin wedding
preparations. They traveled through the night
with very little sleep to quickly visit venues. It
was a bit hard to do so with so little time
because they wanted to get married in just a few
months after Christy graduated with her
Bachelor's Degree. We only had ten months to
plan for an August wedding. We were unable to
find availability, but a date in July was available

so they took it. July 20, 2007 was the date,

which meant we had to roll up our sleeves and

get to work to make it all happen.

With Christy finishing up her senior year

at school, she couldn't do all the preparations

for the wedding, so she left them to me. I never

made any decision without her, and she was so

incredible to work with. If I asked her what she

wanted, she told me and I would work on it. If

she said no to anything, we moved onto what

she wished for. I had saved some money, and

told her I would buy her wedding dress with

what I had set aside. I had a budget, and when

she was able to come home again at Christmas,

we went shopping for a gown.

I loved that time with her. We went to

several boutiques in our area, and I told her she

would know what the perfect dress was when

she found it and saw herself in the mirror. She

had one all picked out but wasn't really sure.

We went to another store, and when she put on

this one particular dress, her face lit up and I

knew that this would be the dress. It was two

cents under budget. The gown was stark white,

and Christy was so proud to wear white. It was

three tiers of lace with a ribbon laced back. It

went off the shoulders with a train that was just

right. The dress was all Christy with just enough

wow factors to it, but nothing over the top.

Christy was not about drawing attention to

herself in any way. She didn't need anything

costly because she knew her worth was not of

anything in this world. Her life was always

about others, not herself. I admired her for the

qualities she possessed, and not only was she

pure in the physical sense, but her heart was also

the same. Christy felt that she was wearing a pure white dress as a testament to her purity. That may seem a little old fashioned to some, but it meant so much to Christy because she made that promise to herself that she would remain pure for her husband. It was also important to her that her husband would do the same.

She chose a veil that clipped into the back of her hair and hung down to the second layer of lace. She looked radiant as she stood in front of the mirror smiling about her selection. I was beaming watching her look over every detail of her choice, and could not wait for the day I had always dreamed of. My wedding was very small, and I didn't have a wedding gown. I believe Christy allowed me to be such a big part of planning her wedding because she knew I was also planning the wedding I would have loved to have had. She was again showing her selflessness and ability to make others happy. She always made me feel so loved all the time.

Because Christy possessed a personality that was witty and hilarious, she would say things to Jeff to get him going. As she was choosing her wedding party, she told us she wanted a Chinese flower girl. We asked her how that was going to happen, and I laughed when Jeff told her she couldn't rent someone's child. Her reply was "watch me." For Christy, we expected her to find a way because she always did. She figured out how to make things happen and was successful almost every time.

We knew there was a family at church that had adopted a little girl from China. Her name was Hannah and her family was very sweet. Christy and I approached them after the morning service, and I began explaining to them that Christy had something to ask. Hannah was about three years old and she was sitting on her dad's shoulders. Christy said that she would love to have Hannah as her flower girl, and they were thrilled with her request. When they looked up at this beautiful little girl and asked her if she'd like to be Christy's flower girl, she replied that she would like to be a flower in a wedding. We all cried happy tears and went out to the car where Jeff was waiting. Christy laughed her hilarious way and told Jeff she got her Chinese flower girl. Jeff just shook his head and smiled because he really had no doubt that this would happen.

~Chapter Twelve~

Christy chose the colors of red, yellow, and orange for the wedding. The theme was China, of course, for the shower and the flower bouquets for the wedding. The bridesmaids would wear deep red gowns with rhinestone necklaces and earrings. Her bridal party included her three best friends, her sister-in-law to be, and her two cousins. Corey's groomsmen would be his three best friends, his brother, and

Christy's two brothers. He also had a little boy

he knew very well that he asked to be the ring

bearer with Hannah, the flower girl.

Pastor Reilly and Corey's good friend

who pastored a church in Iowa jointly led the

ceremony at our home church—the place that

Christy always enjoyed coming back to. It was

refreshing to hear the words of each of them as

they spoke about Corey and Christy. There were

traditional elements implemented in the

ceremony and then there were things that gave it

a personal touch. Christy asked for stringed

instruments to be playing before the ceremony,

and as the bridal party walked down the aisle.

We had a special plan for Christy's entrance that

no one knew about. I had a vision how Christy

would be breathtaking as she took her first steps

through the double doors of the auditorium. I

could see her in my mind with her right arm

looped around her dad's left. I wasn't sure if she

would be smiling as the doors opened or

shedding tears. I knew how she was so happy to

marry Corey, but I also knew how this big day

would fill her with many emotions.

I had seen the movie, *Legends of the*

Fall, which had a beautiful wedding scene in it.

The song that was played in that scene became

one of my favorite pieces of music and it was

entitled "The Wedding." This song began to

play and at a precise moment, the doors were

opened by the ushers as Christy and her dad

entered. Her smile was as bright as ever and her

eyes were fixed on her groom who was waiting

for her at the altar. Her dad had that stoic look

on his face, but his eyes sang a different song.

He held back tears as he escorted his girl down

that aisle to meet his soon to be son-in-law.

When asked who was giving this young lady, he

replied without hesitation that we both did. It

wasn't hard because we knew how much

Christy and Corey loved each other. We also

knew that God had great plans for their lives.

God was the center of their lives as individuals,

and now He would be the center of their

marriage.

Jeff sat down next to me and we listened

as the vows were repeated. At one point Pastor

Reilly had to repeat part of the vows as Christy

began to lose her composure a bit. She managed

to get through them, and the two of them just

continued to smile at each other whispering

back and forth.

Weddings are always so beautiful, and I wonder how often we hear these vows spoken and promised. The wedding vows are commitments to each that should be revered. As I sat and listened to the words my daughter was exchanging with her groom, I began to ponder them a little more than before. The promises of "to have and to hold, from this day forward, for better, for worse, for richer, for poorer, in sickness and in health, until death do us part," are sacred and I knew that these two beautiful people would keep these promises to the end. They didn't care if they were rich or poor, and they knew they would have good times and bad. But the sickness and health part, I don't think they ever put much thought into that; at least not expecting anything bad to happen early on in marriage. The only thing they were truly focusing on at that moment was their future as a married couple and what God had for them.

Corey had a cool plan for the end of the ceremony. He lifted Christy into his arms after he kissed her, and the song "I'm a Believer," began to play loudly as he carried her down the aisle and out of the auditorium. That was Corey! Always making things happy and fun, adding just a little twist to end the ceremony. I was thrilled with how wonderful everything was and how beautiful the entire afternoon went.

Usually, July is very hot in Michigan, but not on that day. It was beautiful, as if we special ordered the weather. The sun was shining without a cloud to be seen, the temperatures were just right, and the humidity was low. The pictures of Christy and her bridesmaids were taken in our backyard before the ceremony and then we went to the park in our community that everyone loves between the wedding and the reception. Pictures were taken by the covered bridge and other beautiful areas in a hurry. The reception was about twenty minutes away, and Christy didn't want to keep her guests waiting. The bridal party jumped into the limo and away they went to begin the celebration of the newlyweds.

The reception was set to begin two hours after the ceremony at a venue that was able to accommodate the large amount of guests that had been invited. Friends and family from out-of-state traveled to be with Corey and Christy on their wedding day. The hall was decorated with Christy's favorite flowers, the Gerbera Daisy. Each table was decorated with a white linen table cloth, red napkins, and one of three

different centerpieces on round mirrors. There
were several votive candles scattered around the
arrangements creating warm, reflecting lighting.

As the guests arrived, and found their
way to their assigned seats, hors d'oeuvres were
served and a non-alcoholic bar was available
with fancy, fruity beverages. Christy and Corey
had decided they did not want alcohol served at
their event which made perfect sense.

As the bridal party made their way in
from the limousine, the guests applauded them.
The bride and groom were beaming with
happiness. They made their way to the head
table, grace was said, and dinner began. There
was the typical fare which included chicken,
beef, vegetables, salad, and rolls. Each guest
was given a fortune cookie with a Bible verse, a
perfect gift from the newlyweds.

After The Matron of Honor, and Best
Man gave their toasts, the music began to play
calling out those who loved to dance. The first
set of songs was for the bride and groom and
they danced to the song "Feels Like Home," by
Chantal Kreviazuk. It was such a pretty song
and such a lovely moment to see my daughter's
eyes light up and her smile as she was taking on
another new role in her life. I stood on the edge
of the dance floor smiling, and feeling that I was
witnessing something very special. I was
looking at a young woman, who I called my
daughter, with so much ahead of her. She would
take on many more roles throughout her life,
and I knew I would continue to encourage her in
anything she would do. This night was
everything I had dreamed of for Christy, and I
was so captivated by her beauty.

Christ with a Y

Once the bridal party finished their dance, Christy and her dad met in the middle of the floor surrounded by those who loved her. Jeff was dressed in a black tuxedo with a matching vest and tie and he looked fantastic. I knew the minute he took Christy into his arms he was toast, and I saw his eyes well up with tears. I could see Christy smiling and teasing him, but I knew her well enough to see the emotion in her face. I am sure they danced to a country song, Christy loved this genre as well as Christian music, but I cannot remember what was played. The beautiful ceremony was captured on video, but the reception was not, unfortunately.

The rest of the evening was spent eating wedding cake, dancing, and laughing with those we loved. We knew we had put on a great party that night, and Christy was happy to be surrounded by everyone who was there. She had found her "Mr. Right" and had become Mrs. Wright that day. She was such a jubilant bride. I was so proud of her for.

They spent the night in a hotel we had reserved for them, and the next day they departed for a honeymoon in Cabo San Lucas, Mexico. They enjoyed their time of relaxation at an all inclusive resort for one week. They took a flight back to Lynchburg, where they would begin a new life together as husband and wife.

~Chapter Thirteen~

Not long after being married, the

yearning for a dog began. Hours of research was

put into action to know which breed would fit

their personalities. It seemed that a yellow lab

would fit them most appropriately, so away they

went to pick out their new puppy. They traveled

a few hours from Lynchburg to see a litter of

new Labrador Retrievers a breeder had

advertised. About this same time the movie

Marley and Me had just been released about a vivacious lab. The story was about a couple who had left the state of Michigan to purchase their first home in Florida. They found a puppy to bring home and all the mischief this little fur ball created was unbelievable. No matter how much furniture this dog destroyed, the family loved him and Marley brought out the best in all of them.

"Molly" came to live with Corey and Christy when she was old enough to be weaned from her mother. She was a sweet, cream-colored canine with big paws that made her clumsy when she ran. She was soft and full of energy. Her black nose was like a piece of coal on a snowman, and her eyes were filled with love. She stole Christy's heart the moment she met her. Puppies are so cute, but as they begin to settle in, they begin to get comfortable. It did

not take long for Molly to make her mark on

The Wright home! Table legs were splintered,

rugs were frayed, cell phones were shredded,

and blankets were dragged down the hallways.

Christy lost dozens of shoes, her socks

mysteriously disappeared, and dog fur filled

every corner of their hardwood floors. This dog

even helped herself to a dish of lasagna from the

stove top fresh out of the oven, and pulled a

thawing chicken out of the sink to eat! She grew

into a great big dog within a short amount of

time. Her tail was thick and wagged nonstop. It

would whip you as she walked by. If anyone

stood in her way as she ran by, they would be

taken down to their knees before they knew it.

Forget about peace and quiet, because this dog

barked endlessly.

They traveled up for a visit so we could
meet Molly not long after they had her. Josh had
just gotten a puppy, too: a miniature pinscher he
named Danke'. He had gotten a female and
wanted her to have a name that wasn't too
feminine, so since her breed was of German
descent and means thank you, it was
appropriate. When both puppies met at our
house, which was pretty new, Molly initiated it
right away with a big puddle right in the
doorway of our somewhat formal dining room.
Our new light beige carpet had a nice big yellow
spot. I let out a huge "NOOOOO," and everyone
knew immediately what had happened. I'm not
sure if Corey and Christy were upset that this
happened or if they found it funny. I'm guessing
the latter. The two dogs got along well
considering their size difference, and both Josh

and Christy were proud of their new dogs. Jeff was not a fan of having pets, but from then on we had furry guests on every visit. That was great for me because I have always been a huge animal lover!

Of course, traveling back and forth from Virginia to Michigan with a dog became more difficult as Molly grew. I struggled with Christy being so far away and called her every day. When Christy decided to attend college in another state, I knew it was a pretty good possibility my little girl would never return home, except on visits. Christy had a good job and Corey was still attending school as well as working for the university in the cabinet shop. I would call her at the bank, where she worked, and she would answer the phone so professionally, stating the establishment's name.

She would then clearly pronounce her name, Christy Wright. It was so hard to get used to her new married name. As soon as she would hear my voice, she would always just say "MOM," like she always did. I wish I could play an audio of her shouting this out because it always made me laugh. Sometimes annoying my kids was fun but they loved to call me a nag when I did. Oh well, it was fun to annoy her.

The newlyweds were busy everyday with work, school, extra side jobs, a puppy, and remodeling their home on Oakdale Drive. They were so in love with each other and dedicated to figuring out their new lives together. Corey and Christy were continually praying about where God would lead them. They were waiting to finish their degrees before making any big decisions. They knew to leave it in the Lord's hands, but they were also anxious for His direction to come quickly.

I loved listening to Christy talk about her future because she had so much wisdom and a huge heart for sharing her passion for how God worked through everything in her life. She was a dedicated follower of Christ and made no decision without seeking His desires for her life.

Jeff and I tried to visit as often as we could, and made a decision to find a vacation spot to meet Corey and Christy so they, too, could get away a little bit. We found a place in Myrtle Beach, South Carolina, that we fell in love with one summer, and knew this is where our vacations occurred in the upcoming years.

~Chapter Fourteen~

So many things were going on in our lives during the next few years. I made a decision to go to college for a career in the medical field. I went to a local community college and became a Certified Medical Assistant. I thought nursing would be what I wanted, but God had something else planned for me. Of course, these things do not always make sense until you look back and then you see how

His hand was in it all. I know that sometimes our tiny minds cannot understand the bigger picture because we are not wired to comprehend the things of God.

In May of 2009, I finished my schooling as a Certified Medical Assistant, and Christy finished her Master's Degree work. We traveled to Liberty University to see Christy receive her Master of Arts degree as well as Corey attaining his Bachelor's Degree. It was a bit different from Christy's undergrad ceremony back in May of 2007. The founder of Liberty, Rev. Jerry Falwell, had passed away just before graduation. It was so sad for all these students because he was loved on campus. He was always present and waved at everyone as he drove through the university in his black SUV. He was taken through the streets of the university in a horse-drawn hearse lined with people along the way. It was a warm, Virginia day as the horses slowly made their way to the steps of the church on the campus where the service took place. Newt Gingrich was the guest speaker for that graduation. He did a wonderful job, especially, considering what had just happened. Although it was a sad time, the graduates were still honored and celebrated their accomplishments.

Josh traveled down with us this time to see his sister and brother-in-law graduate. It was a great day of family celebrations. For this ceremony, the speaker was Ben Stein, another man with a great speech at a Liberty graduation. The weather was just like it had been two years prior for Christy's first graduation ceremony. We were thankful for no rain.

Christ with a y

Once all the festivities were finished, we celebrated Corey and Christy at a restaurant we grew to love in the area. We went to church the next day and took pictures under the flowering tree in Corey and Christy's front yard. She said that tree was one of the reasons they fell in love with their ranch style house. Under the tree was a little cement bench, and in front of the house on each side of the porch were holly bushes that were deadly. Every time we worked on cleaning them out, we were stabbed by the barbs. We took a lot of cute photos that afternoon with our sunburned noses and cheeks. Even early mornings in central Virginia were warm and sunny during springtime. The sun kissed us all that day as we watched two very special graduates smiling about their achievements.

Christy was so much more than I could have asked for in a daughter. I was still amazed at how wise she had become at such a young age. I adored watching her with her friends and how she was able to talk to a stranger so effortlessly. She was given such a gift that continually developed and made her special. When we gave Christy gift cards for restaurants while she was at school, she would give them to people in need when she saw them on the streets, but she would share her love for Jesus first. There was a time she wrote something about smiling at people because she said you never know what's going on in their life. She said someone may have recently found out some bad news or that they were diagnosed with cancer. Christy always put others first no matter what. There were so many people she did things for, and I'm sure I don't even know the half of them. I loved that she never expected anything in return for her sweet actions. So often people hope to be given back something for the things they have done, but I do not believe that ever crossed Christy's mind. She simply wanted to serve others, which was an impressive quality to me.

When she met people that didn't know her, she would begin talking to them by introducing herself. When she said her name, she would tell people her name was spelled "Christ" with a "y". It was an impressive way to get someone's attention to begin a conversation about Christ and to see how Christy's heart was seen through her actions. Her smile was so infectious that no one could help interacting with her and learning what gave her that smile.

She was never afraid to share her love for Jesus, and I believe everyone that knew her realized she did just by seeing her smile and talking with her for a few minutes.

When I learned of Christy's way of introducing herself, it became clear to me why I was drawn to the spelling of her name the evening before her birth. Once again, watching how God weaves our stories through time continues to put a smile on my face. He blessed us with this daughter and then through her life she was becoming a huge blessing to so many. She saw in her name the ability to begin a conversation about Christ that would ease her words into an introduction to her Savior.

~Chapter Fifteen~

Christy found a lump in her breast one day in the spring that worried her terribly. I never liked getting a phone call from Christy when something was bothering her because I could only talk to her over the phone. I told her to make an appointment with the doctor and eased her mind by telling her it was more than likely nothing to worry over.

During the doctor's visit, she was examined and sent for a biopsy. The results came back as a benign cyst. I wished I would have been able to travel down to Lynchburg to be with her, but it was not possible because of my schooling.

Even though this was considered a benign cyst, it remained in the back of my mind that it was something more than the test results revealed. There was no history of breast cancer in our family except for a great-great aunt on my mom's side. Christy cried about this experience and grew more anxious than I liked. She did not accept the results very well. Eventually, she put it out of her mind and all was well. At least that was how she made me feel about it.

Christ with a y

I finished my certification testing on the first of July upon finishing my externship in the internal medicine department of a clinic. Just before our planned vacation to Myrtle Beach with Christy and Corey, I was offered a position in the pediatric department of this office. They agreed to let me wait until after we returned. I was excited that I was offered this job, and anxious to use my recently learned skills as a Medical Assistant.

In August, we met Corey and Christy in North Myrtle Beach. We had a two bedroom condo on a golf course that was perfect. The only thing was one of the bedrooms had two twin beds. That was Corey and Christy's room. They didn't care, they were just happy to be away on vacation. Our favorite beach was about twenty minutes south at the state park. We had plenty of fun things to do, but my favorite place was right on the beach. The others in our party were not so excited about spending hours in the sun. Our first visit in the ocean was not too cool for Corey. Five minutes in and a jellyfish stung his leg. He was only knee-deep in the water and he fell victim fast. Always the good sport about everything, Corey didn't let it ruin our time. He just went with it and spent the rest of the day having fun.

I noticed Christy looked somewhat different as soon as I saw her. She was much heavier than when we had seen her in May. I was concerned about her, and while the two of us were at the beach alone, I said something to her about it. She reacted quickly and was upset with me. She had been telling me about her weight gain and was trying to change her eating habits as well as swim. She was taking Molly for walks after work each day, but it really wasn't doing much. I felt horrible making her feel bad, but I couldn't help needing to talk to her about it. She got up from under our cabana and walked down the beach alone. When she returned she had a shell in her hand and told me it was a forgiveness shell and that she forgave me. That was Christy, always making sure to forgive anyone. That was one of those days where I wanted to grab the words I had spoken and stuff them back in my mouth. It was too late, though, I had hurt her.

This vacation was something that I will never forget because we were two couples having a great time at the beach. We did everything together, and the best thing was our decision to parasail. It was so much fun, but we were a little nervous after reading all the rules and things that could happen. Once we paid for our trip out into the Atlantic Ocean, we were all in. Christy was quite nervous about doing this, but I think she thought if her mom was doing it, she better take a deep breath and go.

We took an inflatable banana boat pulled by a jet ski out to the boat and then boarded. We went as pairs, and Jeff and I went first. The higher we climbed, the more peaceful it felt. Looking down toward the water was a little frightening, but the ocean was calm and serene. We were pulled in after a little bit and dragged through the water before landing on the boat. Christy and Corey went after us, and they laughed the entire time. They, too, were dragged through the water before coming in. The banana boat took us back to shore, but instead of a nice landing, he flung us around and we all fell off the raft and slid through the pebbles of the shallow beach. It was a great experience that made us all happy we decided to do it.

Corey and Christy soon left, and we continued the last few days of the trip alone. We were ready to continue vacationing like this whenever possible, hoping our sons would be able to join us in the future. We needed to continually make plans like these so we would have new adventures together and memories to share.

Just a few weeks later in early September, Corey's sister was getting married in western Michigan. Christy and Corey were in the wedding and flew into the airport near our home. We picked them up and took them out to where the wedding was. Because we were invited but went early, we made a little vacation out of the weekend. Christy looked even heavier to me than she did two weeks earlier at the beach. I'd never seen her look so big, but she seemed more swollen than overweight. Her cheeks were quite puffy, and she just did not look well. I know it bothered her immensely to be overweight, but we couldn't figure out what was going on.

The weekend went well and we drove back to our area to drop the two of them off at the airport to go back to Virginia. I hated seeing Christy leave again as it seemed to get harder for me to be away from her. I had accepted that she was married and living a new life with her love, but I missed her terribly all the time. Maybe deep down I knew something was brewing within her, but couldn't comprehend what it was.

The first indication that something wasn't right besides the weight gain was when Christy began to have flu like symptoms when they returned home from Michigan. She went to the doctor several times and was told she had a virus. Her throat hurt, she was exhausted all the time, and just didn't have the energy to do much. After continually trying things to feel better that didn't work, she returned to the doctor. She was given a round of antibiotics which helped a little, but once the medication was finished, the symptoms returned.

I was now working for two pediatricians at the clinic and was worried about Christy. Getting back into the groove of working was challenging for me. I was working more hours

than I had hoped, but really had no choice.
Being far away from each other with her being
sick was difficult. I asked the doctors questions
about Christy's symptoms whenever I could, but
it's not easy to diagnose someone when they
aren't in the office in front of a doctor.

I began missing Christy and we had no
plans to see them again until Christmas. I told
her I would help pay for a ticket so she could
come up to see us. She found a flight that was a
great value over the Columbus Day weekend.
Working at a bank gave her this day off. She
came up on that Friday evening through
Monday afternoon for a quick visit.

Our weekend was just a time to rest and
be together. All was well, but Christy's sore
throat and exhaustion was evident. It was not
unusual that she wanted to catch a little shut eye

during this quick weekend trip. It seemed like she was feeling a little better compared to our conversations over the past month and a half.

We went to church that Sunday and everyone was so excited to see her. Christy loved our church and really never found another one like it where she lived. There were many places to worship surrounding them in their area, but not one that compared to the place she called her home. People were happy to see Christy, and she was thrilled to see so many friends. They hugged her and snapped photos together.

I really do not remember much about the rest of that day, but on Monday when Christy was to return to Virginia, a whole new scenario was

about to begin that would change our lives
forever.

Christy's flight was late in the afternoon,
so the two of us went to one of her favorite
restaurants for lunch. Everything was fine until
we began eating. Christy began to feel
nauseated and was unable to eat. Since it was
normal for Christy to have anxiety of flying and
leaving us, I assumed this is what the problem
was. She continued to feel worse, so once I was
finished eating, we paid the bill, and left to go
home.

We hung around the house while Christy
relaxed, and then I drove her to the airport. I
hated that day because not only was she leaving
to go back to Virginia but also, she was sick.
There was no way she would stay here because
she was so dedicated to her job and her husband.

Christ with a Y

I knew she was torn, but she was missing Corey
and Molly.

Of course, the trip home couldn't have
been a usual one. The plane had problems and
was delayed, and then when it landed at the
airport in North Carolina, the flight to
Lynchburg was canceled due to engine
problems. At this point, Christy began having
severe pain in her lower right groin area. It was
difficult for her to walk, and she just needed to
get home. This pain came out of nowhere and it
was intense.

Because Christy had a husband that
would do anything for his bride, he drove down
to the airport in Charlotte to get her and bring
her home. On top of being very sick, Christy
wanted to get home so she wouldn't have to call
off work. This is how Christy was with

everything she did. It is what she was taught, but took it very seriously. There were so many times I knew Christy should have stayed home from school, work, or church, but she never would. If there wasn't a fever, she would muster up the strength to follow through whatever it was she had committed to doing.

There was a little more to this night, as Christy met a young man that attended school at Virginia Tech University in Blacksburg. He was on his way home and couldn't get there either. Corey and Christy went out of their way to take this gentleman back to school before heading home. Needless to say, it didn't phase them at all to do this, nor did they probably ever tell anyone. They always did random acts of kindness for so many people. God had put these

two together in a special way, and watching
them grow together was so beautiful.

It was very early Tuesday morning when
Corey and Christy finally drove up to their
house, and they were worn out. Christy ended
up staying home from work because of being so
tired and very sick. She was in a lot of pain, and
the same symptoms from September were
reoccurring. She went to her family doctor and
again was treated for a virus. Her complaint to
her doctor was shortness of breath and right hip
pain. She was given an inhaler for asthma and
medication for acid reflux. An X-ray of her hip
was taken where some "spots" were noticed,
and an appointment with an orthopedist was
made for January 10, 2010. I couldn't believe
how far away that appointment was for someone
who was so sick and couldn't be diagnosed with

anything specific. With the indication of something noticeable in the X-ray, it seemed there should have been more urgency.

I would persistently ask the pediatricians I was working for what their thoughts were about Christy's symptoms. At this time in our office, we had a seventeen year old patient that was having pain, and he was later diagnosed with a Ewing Sarcoma in his hip. I was feeling a bit like this mother whom I had not met as she desperately sought a doctor to help her son. Helplessness was beginning to overwhelm me as I had a hard time knowing what to do, and it was hard to concentrate on my job. All I could think about was how I could help my girl.

I unceasingly called Christy every moment I had because being so far away from her made me feel helpless. My daughter was very focused and motivated to continue going to work every day although she was suffering. She had her own office now on the second floor, and she loved having her own desk. She dealt with people in the area that were wealthy and helped them with their banking needs. Her title was a Wealth Management Associate, and she was so proud of that.

During this time, Christy would try to go grocery shopping with Corey, and she could barely make it down one aisle of the store without having to sit on the floor to catch her breath and alleviate the pain in her hip. I know this was hard for Corey to watch and he struggled not knowing what to do. They were only twenty-four years old. How was she incapable of not making it down one aisle? She kept pushing herself and trying everything to help herself feel better. We suggested a massage, and she made an appointment. This only intensified the pain and made her back hurt terribly. I was really getting concerned, and I contemplated a trip to Lynchburg. I had only been working at my new job for a few months and was still training and testing, so it was not something I could easily do.

As Thanksgiving was approaching, Christy's health was declining more and more. She was working alone the Friday after Thanksgiving and was in so much pain. She put her phone on the floor and covered up with a blanket waiting for phone calls. She made it through the hours she was scheduled to work and went home. A few days later, on November 29, 2009, Corey was outside raking leaves. I was able to talk Christy into going to the hospital emergency room as she was explaining how bad she felt. I called Corey to ask him to take her because I was afraid she would not go once we hung up from our conversation. He agreed and took her to Lynchburg General Hospital. She was tested and admitted to the cardiac unit where she was diagnosed with Pericarditis, which is fluid surrounding the heart. She also had Graves Disease, also known as hyperthyroidism. This is an autoimmune disorder which attacks the thyroid causing more hormone than the body needs. She was put on a high dose of Ibuprofen, Lopressor, and Colchicine to relieve the fluid around her heart. A medication called PTU was prescribed to her for the Graves Disease. Jeff and I left to go down to be with Christy and help them with Molly. Christy was resting comfortably when we arrived and laughing with us in her private room.

Christy had a client at the bank, Mr. Stroobants, who always called her "Christy, my girl". He was a very wealthy businessman and philanthropist that seemed to like Christy. The cardiac unit at Lynchburg General was named after him. Christy thought it was quite amazing to be here because she really liked this gentleman. He seemed to engage in conversation with his favorite banker in a friendly manner, and Christy enjoyed that.

Jeff and I went to the house, cleaned it all up, and made enough food to put in the freezer for about a month. We took care of that crazy dog in between our long visits at the hospital until Christy was released on December fourth. She was advised to stay home from work until the fluid around her heart was gone. This was not something Christy took lightly, and worked from home as much as she could. Her bosses were very understanding and just wanted her to recover quickly.

Christy seemed to be getting better but slowly. Her next appointment with the cardiologist showed some improvement; she was told to continue the medication, but she was not to return to work just yet. She was still unable to walk very far and did little at home. Christy liked to read, so she sat in her chair relaxing with good books. She received a ton of cards and well wishes while she was recuperating. Molly kept her company, and Corey went to work each day at Liberty. Christy proofread Corey's papers for school as well, which she enjoyed doing for him.

I made my daily phone calls and consultations with the doctors I was working for. Continual prayers were being said for Christy to heal. As a mother, there are just things you know, and I knew something was really wrong with Christy. She wasn't bouncing back from this, and I began thinking about what was happening. I never wanted to assume what I feared, but deep down I was beginning to ponder what the future was going to be for her.

Corey and Christy were planning on coming up for Christmas to see their families. They would generally give both families their time when traveling up for holidays. As the middle of December was approaching, they had to make the decision to stay in Lynchburg as Christy's health was in question. It was a hard decision because I know they wanted to make the trip as much as we wanted them to.

We packed a great big box of wrapped Christmas gifts for Corey, Christy, and Molly and sent them down. We wanted them to have their gifts to open on Christmas so they would enjoy celebrating together in their house.

Christy stayed in her comfortable recliner chair that sat next to her bookshelf that Corey made for her while they were dating. She had so many books and Corey was mastering his building skills. He was so happy to make that work of art for her, and she loved it. It consisted of many shelves and was stained a beautiful, rich color. He had drilled enough holes into the back so each shelf could be adjusted to accommodate various sized books and decorations.

While they were opening their presents from all of us, Christy was uncomfortable. She sat in her chair curled up wearing her pajama pants and a T-shirt. They were sending us pictures as they opened each gift. I could tell Christy was not herself and that she was feeling poorly. She was beginning to spend much of her time in a hot bath. She said it was the only thing that helped her feel better. New symptoms had popped up at this point. There was a bulge protruding from the upper right area, just under her ribs, and she could not stand up straight.

~Chapter Sixteen~

On Saturday, December 26, 2009, I called Christy to see how she was doing. She was crying and was terribly afraid to go to the hospital. She was in uncontrollable pain and unable to stand up without being bent over. I begged her to go to the hospital, but she insisted on staying home. I called Corey and told him my thoughts and he agreed. After hanging up the phone, I was in deep thought as to how

Corey would get Christy into the car to take her to the emergency room, so I called him back. I suggested they call for an ambulance, and he agreed. He called 911, and they came quickly to transport her to the same hospital she had been admitted to a month earlier. It was very hard for them to get Christy into the vehicle with the amount of pain she was in and her inability to stand.

After a short time in the ER, Corey called me, and the words that came from his mouth sent me into almost a panic. I felt like I couldn't breathe, nor could I even think straight. It was a call I dreaded but knew would come. Corey's words were: "Karen, they are checking her for cancer."

I dropped my cell phone to the floor where I was lying on the sofa. Jeff knew the news was bad and he picked up the phone to

talk to Corey. He was in disbelief and told

Corey we would be down as soon as we could.

Once Jeff hung up the phone, he got me up from

the couch. He said that we would leave for

Virginia in the morning. We packed our bags

once I had gotten myself together. I felt like I

was in a dream and just threw things in the

suitcase that didn't even make sense. I didn't

care how it was packed, I just grabbed things.

My limbs were lifeless and my mind was in a

fog. This wasn't supposed to be happening. She

was such a vibrant young lady with all these

plans ahead of her. This is the girl that was

living her entire life for her Savior. My daughter

was the one who I shared everything with and

adored. She was who would take care of me in

my old age one day and give us grandchildren,

biological and adopted babies.

She was admitted with a fever, extreme

lower back and hip pain, and abdominal pain

near her liver. She was put on Morphine for the

inflammation and fever, Lortab and Dilaudid for

pain, and Lovenox to prevent pulmonary

embolisms. There were many tests ordered, such

as a CT scan of her hip and abdominal area, an

MRI, urinalysis, and a bone scan.

~Chapter Seventeen~

The morning of Sunday, December 27th,

we left to head south. It was a typical Michigan

winter day that started out with ice and snow.

As we headed down I-75 towards the Ohio

Turnpike, the roads became very slippery. We

were driving our truck, and I was already filled

with anxiety. We drove past accident after

accident, and eventually saw a horse trailer that

had crashed with the horse lying on the road and

people all around it. As we passed that awful

site, we began to spin sideways, and I felt as

though I couldn't take anymore. I began to cry,

but Jeff pulled the vehicle out of the spin

without ever losing his nerve. A few more miles

down the turnpike and the sun began to shine,

melting the icy road. I knew that God had heard

me and knew I needed assurance that He would

get us to Christy safely. The duration of the

drive to the hospital in Lynchburg was spent in

silence as thoughts raced through our minds. It

was dark when we entered the hospital parking

lot and there was snow on the ground but there

were also pansies lining the entrance to the main

doors.

When we walked into the hospital room

where Corey sat with Christy, we could see how

much pain our beautiful daughter was in. She

was on large amounts of pain medication, but it didn't seem to be helping her. It did, however, make her hallucinate. There were times she would tell us things and then realize they didn't make sense. Her best story was the green bean with a smile that was always on her leg. She would see that little bean continually and ask us all if we could see it. She would be talking to us, and all of sudden, out of nowhere, she would get wide eyed and whisper those words as if it could hear her. As soon as we would laugh a little, she would realize he really wasn't there.

The one thing that would send Christy into tears was the touch of strangers. This was something Christy always despised. She felt that no one had the right to touch her without her permission. There were so many medical personnel coming and going from her room.

Constant needle pokes and tests that I knew hurt her made me cringe. Although Christy was twenty-four years old, I believe she reverted into a childlike mindset when it came to the experiences she was enduring. It broke my heart to see her in this condition, and nothing seemed to take the pain down to a tolerable level.

She was a young girl in so much pain that she had to have assistance in the bathroom to do the simplest of tasks. Corey took great care of Christy, and he did it all with such compassion and love. Her hair was very long and thick, so we had to wash it for her in the sink. It was so hard for her to bend over to do this as the pain in her abdomen was excruciating.

Later that evening when Jeff and I went back to the house to take care of Molly, I knew I would have trouble eating. All the feelings I had

choked down from our first day with Christy

would eventually come out. We went to eat

dinner at a restaurant, and it was basically a

disaster. I ordered what I thought I was hungry

for. After one bite, I began to cry. Jeff had tears

in his eyes as well, and we really had no words

for each other. He was eventually able to soothe

and comfort me, but I was unable to eat. This

would continue for the next week. I felt like

everyone was looking at us, but they really

weren't. This experience taught me how we

never know what is happening in someone's

life. It's easy to form an opinion quickly before

knowing what is actually going on in people

around us. Here we were, twelve hours away

from home, dealing with something we didn't

know how to handle. With all the strangers

passing us in the restaurants, grocery stores, and hospital none of them had a clue what we were dealing with, nor the burden we were carrying. It truly made me see people and the world in a different light.

We spent the night at Corey and Christy's house, and being newlyweds, the house was not completely furnished at this point. In the spare bedroom was a twin bed that was custom built for Corey when he was young. The bed was built on top of a six drawer dresser, and Jeff slept up there. We had brought a twin mattress upstairs from the bedroom in the basement for me to sleep on in the same room. Molly, oh Molly! She was so happy to have someone home with her that she was all over me! She was nibbling on my hair and trying to get onto the mattress with me. Did I mention this was a *twin* mattress and she probably weighed seventy pounds? I honestly believe that God knew Jeff and I needed an icebreaker, and he gave it to us with Molly. We laughed and laughed at the antics of this dog until we fell asleep. I had a dog sleeping almost on my head the entire night.

During the next week, Christy continued to have pain that was never adequately relieved. The green bean with a smile was visiting often, and Christy couldn't get up from her bed except to use the bathroom. She needed assistance with anything when she was up.

The results from the tests began to come back revealing some things, but not matching any of the cancers they were testing for. The bone scan results showed spots on her right hip, the lower thoracic, and upper lumbar regions of

the spine. The MRI showed nothing in her head
or limbs. Blood work was positive for anemia,
and the CT scan confirmed the bone scan
results.

The medical staff was baffled as to what
this was and couldn't pinpoint a diagnosis. We
held off saying it was cancer out loud because
we really weren't given that, but we knew the
doctors were certain it was. They were testing
for soft tissue cancers but were coming up with
negative results.

A liver biopsy was ordered, and it is one
day I will never forget. Christy was nervous
about this procedure because she would be
alone in the imaging room. The doctor inserted
a very large, long needle directly into Christy's
liver with no anesthesia. She was slightly
sedated, but not enough to take away her

anxiety. Corey and I were able to go into the
area where the doctor was looking at the scan.
This doctor was another one of Christy's
customers at the bank, but we didn't discuss that
with him. I remember his face when he looked
at us and said Christy was a very sick girl. The
results showed many lesions on her liver, but
the biopsy results were inconclusive as they
were only able to retrieve necrotic tissue.

Christy was so ill and made a very
strong statement that she did not want any
visitors. This was so difficult because so many
people loved Christy, and they were worried
about her. Her most cherished friends tried their
hardest to visit, but this only made Christy more
anxious. As more and more medical staff came
into the room and touched her just out of
kindness, tears would well up in her eyes. She

just wanted to be alone and concentrate on what was happening to her. She was scared and unsure of her future. It was also obvious that she was not only concerned for herself but also for Corey, Jeff, and me.

The decision was made to transfer Christy to The University of Virginia Hospital in Charlottesville. The other alternative was Duke University in North Carolina. UVA was a bit closer to Oakdale Drive, so we opted for this hospital. Arrangements were made for the ambulance to transport her once a bed was found for her. It was a wet, dreary New Year's Eve when we left Lynchburg.

Corey bought a Teddy Bear for Christy from the hospital store that was dressed like a doctor. This bear accompanied Christy in the ambulance. The driver and the attendant treated

Christy with great care. She was given anti-anxiety medication before we left Lynchburg to keep her calm and comfortable. She was continually monitored throughout the journey north, and the paramedic told Christy a lot of stories.

I have serious motion sickness when traveling anywhere but the front seat where I can look directly out the windshield. I cannot read or look down much when traveling, and taking medication only puts me to sleep. I was very apprehensive about riding in the back of an ambulance, but I knew Christy would want me with her. Corey and Jeff followed in their vehicles, and I kept looking out the large back windows to make sure they were with us. We were all so tired, and it seemed there was no end to what was happening.

Corey had gone home to kennel Molly and take care of the house before we left. Everything was taken care of, and we had no idea where this would all lead. Everyone in Michigan was concerned and continually praying for Christy. She received get well cards everyday which she loved to open. It helped take her mind off things.

When we arrived at the hospital, it was very late in the afternoon. The hospital in Lynchburg was new and very beautiful. Christy was in a large private room on the oncology floor with her own bathroom. There was comfortable furniture for all of us and access to anything we needed. Now we were entering a much older hospital that was unfamiliar and very different from Lynchburg General. Christy was taken to a semi-private room with a woman with throat problems in the bed closest to the door. I knew my daughter would not be comfortable in this atmosphere, and she began to hyperventilate. Not because of her roommate, but because she was a very private girl. The Interns, Fellows, and Doctors began coming in continually asking question after question over and over again. One Fellow in particular was ordering tests, and her bedside manner was terrible. Christy began to cry, and this did not go over well with her dad. He took the young doctor out into the hallway, and carefully but firmly explained what Christy had been enduring and how fragile she was. I loved that my husband was protecting his child in such a sensitive manner. Within an hour or so, Christy was transferred to a private room just down the hall. She was admitted to the

Hematology/Oncology Unit.

Even with all the medical schooling I

had just completed, there were things that just

didn't register in my mind. I think it was a

coping mechanism for me to avoid reading into

too much. I knew all the medical terms, but

didn't absorb them completely. This was so new

to all of us, and the number one priority was to

keep Christy comfortable. It wasn't an easy

task as she continued to be in a great deal of

pain waiting for a diagnosis.

Corey was given a rollaway bed right

next to Christy's, and he stayed with her every

single night. Jeff and I left to search for a hotel,

which we found about ten minutes away from

the hospital. This would be our home-away-

from-home for eleven days. When we would

arrive at the hospital each morning, Corey would go to our room to shower and rest for a little while. He also traveled back to Lynchburg often to check the mail, take care of the house and check on Molly who was doing just fine in her kennel. Corey would return to be with his bride after a few hours.

The staff at UVA became extremely kind to Christy once they began understanding her situation. More tests were ordered, and some progress was being made. An ultrasound was done on her legs to rule out blood clots, and another CT scan of her abdomen and chest to check for any new developments. They started her on intravenous iron therapy for the anemia, Heparin (a blood thinner) and magnesium.

The doctors had begun speculating that a rather large mass on the right atrium of her heart had metastasized to her liver, hip, and spine. They also found nodules in her lungs. The discussion was now to either do a biopsy of her heart or liver. The possibility of removing the mass from her heart was also tentatively planned. All this was happening so quickly at this point, and Christy was continually leaving her room for these numerous tests.

~Chapter Eighteen~

On January 3, 2010, Christy had an

echocardiogram, and we were able to view the

mass in the atrium of her heart. It was so hard to

understand all of this, and devastating to say the

least. How did Christy have all of these areas

affected without us ever knowing? I began to

reflect on all the appointments and tests we had

gone through over the years. Many of Christy's

symptoms were in the areas most affected by the

spots, nodules, and masses that were appearing in all of the tests. All we could do was rely on our Lord to help us through this. Christy, although anxious, was always talking about how God would remain faithful to her. She would rely on her faith to carry her through these days that were not expected for such a young, vibrant woman.

In Christy's teen years she would always tell me that she would die of cancer by the time she was twenty-eight-years old. I would look at her and think, "What is she talking about? Why would she think that would happen to her?" I reassured her that she would be fine, and I doubted that would happen. She would just smile and tell me it was going to happen. She wasn't able to see into her future, but she had this burning feeling for a long time. Imagine what was going through my mind at this time.

Having liver issues plays a role in the temperature of the body. Christy was always hot, so hot that the temperature in her room was set at fifty-five degrees and she was still hot. The rest of us froze and had to layer our clothing. This gave Jeff and me and opportunity to go into Charlottesville to purchase some cooler, more comfortable clothing for our patient. This is when Christy began sporting The UVA Cavaliers clothing. We bought her shorts and shirts. She was happy with the purchase and proud to be wearing some sporty outfits.

I was beginning to miss my home, my sons, and my dog—Buddy. I talked to my mom and to my very close friends everyday. There was so much love for Christy, and everyone was doing so much to let her know that and feel it.

People began to raise money for Christy and

Corey, and reached out to Jeff and me. There

were so many emotions hitting us everyday. We

would cry because we were horrified by what

was happening, and then we would cry because

we had such a network of love. We could see

God working through things and be filled with

more emotion than we ever knew existed. If we

needed something, we didn't even have to ask

and it was taken care of because God always

takes care of the tiniest details.

The days were long and contained so

much anticipation as we sat with Christy. We

were still waiting for test results to get the actual

diagnosis. Parents were in the hallways and

waiting areas crying for their children who were

even more ill than Christy. So much consoling

was happening each day for others on the hospital floor.

A giant pink banner was made for Christy with a Bible verse from 2 Samuel 22:2-3 on it: "And he said, The Lord is my rock, and my fortress, and my deliverer; The God of my rock; in him will I trust: he is my shield, and the horn of my salvation, my high tower, and my refuge, my Savior; thou savest me from violence." Signatures from all the people that loved Christy from our church were surrounding the sweet words of the Bible. We hung it on the wall so Christy could see it, and it sparked conversation with anyone that walked into Christy's room. Even the visitors of patients on that floor would come in and comment on it. This was another way that Christy could share her faith with others, and she did. Little Miss

Christ with a "Y" was at it again, even though she was ailing.

As the medications were finally beginning to help take Christy's pain to a more tolerable level, she began hearing voices that would say, "Come here." It was difficult for me to listen to these things because they were very strange. I knew the medicine was strong and giving her hallucinations. It was eerie for Christy to hear this, feeling she was being called to Heaven. It made her cry and she asked me what I thought about those words. My daughter was a very special girl. She had qualities about her that I had never experienced in anyone before. Her relationship with Christ was the most beautiful thing. She truly put Him first in her life and would do anything to elevate Him. When I walked away, I felt tears well up in my eyes and sadness overtake my heart. I had to

keep smiling and staying strong for Christy in

her midst. It was never easy to come up with the

right thing to say when these situations popped

up. I believe my daughter heard this call, and

chose to comfort her with words that will

remain between us.

~Chapter Nineteen~

On the fourth of January it was decided

that Christy needed a blood transfusion. She

didn't take to this very well and had a lot of

questions. Her body was unable to replenish all

the blood that was being taken for labs. After

agreeing to the transfusion, she received the A+

blood. Her color immediately changed from

pale to rosy and she felt much better. I was

astonished of the power of this transfusion. The

swelling in her legs diminished, and it seemed

as though we were making some progress in

alleviating some of the annoying symptoms she

had been experiencing.

The results from the echocardiogram

showed the fluid around her heart had cleared

up. An EKG was ordered prior to the biopsy on

her heart that would take place the next day. We

laughed when Christy made a special request for

food from one of her favorite restaurants

because she was having major heart surgery. We

would have gotten her anything she wanted no

matter what. She made everyone laugh, even

when we thought we couldn't.

At 1:30 p.m. on January 5, 2010, Christy

had her procedure done. She returned at 5 p.m.

with a small bandage on her neck. The doctors

who performed the "major heart surgery" came

to the room a little later. They seemed pleased with what they had retrieved and would let us know the results soon.

It was so overwhelming as we watched our daughter suffer in so much pain, and we were still not sure what the exact diagnosis was. We had to be strong for her and comfort her fears. There were so many things we had to do to keep each other's spirits up, too. Corey needed us as much as Christy did. The honeymoon phase of their marriage had not yet passed, and they were very much in love. I am sure they never pondered over their vows at this point. All their plans and dreams were at a standstill now. All I could think about was how they stood before the Lord and recited the words" in sickness and in health." Do we really relish these words when we are standing there looking into each other's eyes? I know that Christy and Corey did. I know they took their marriage vows seriously and promised to keep them until death separated them. There was no clue to any of us that only two years later they would possibly be facing reality of those words.

Charlottesville became a new place to explore as we needed to get things for Christy and find restaurants to eat at. The University of Virginia was beautiful, and it was nice to get away from the hospital a little bit. Whatever Christy needed or wanted, we made sure to get it.

While we were out shopping, there were things that happened that day that showed Jeff and me that God was with us and telling us to trust Him. We knew God wanted us to know that He was with us. I am always fascinated with how He puts people into our path to make us smile and see His work. We didn't even share our story with anyone and they just seemed to know. We stopped at a tiny barber shop so Jeff could get an overdue haircut. The woman who took care of him told him there was no charge for her services. Our lunch was paid for at the restaurant we visited after doing some shopping. By the time we returned to the hospital, we were both emotional and talked about it for a few minutes. Once containing our tears, we headed to Christy's room, still with no results from all the tests.

The reality of how sick Christy really began to set in with her. She was mostly optimistic, but had her times of great sadness. Whenever I helped her with a shower, it would be extremely arduous. Her hair was still difficult to do, and she was unable to stand in the shower for very long. We managed to do the best we could, and once she was back in bed she would be drained. It took a long time for her hair to dry but she always felt better after freshening up and getting a new, clean outfit on. She lived in shorts and T-shirts because of being so hot all the time.

Christy was beginning to lose a lot of weight, and her appetite was slim. Whatever she wanted to eat, we would always rush out and get. Her desire to eat sometimes would only last about fifteen minutes, and once past that threshold, it was hard for her to eat anything.

Cards and flowers began to come in for Christy, which made her smile. She received a box filled with cake pops, a photo album, CD's with music, gift cards, and money. Christy was so excited and humbled by the kindness of her

friends. She loved opening the mail and wanted

to send a thank you note to each person. She

asked for us to get her some note cards to send

to people, and she tried to write but realized

how overwhelming that would be for her.

~Chapter Twenty~

On January 7, 2010 at 4:45 p.m., the
Oncologist and two other doctors came into to
Christy's room with her diagnosis and
prognosis. I don't know how we all really felt at
that moment. We had been waiting for so long
to find out what was really going on with
Christy and why she was so sick. We really
knew all along what it was, but when they

walked into the room, I wasn't sure I wanted to now hear their findings.

The results were matched to a very rare cancer in the outer lining of the blood vessels called Hepatic Epithelioid Hemangioendothelioma. This horrible disease, not many have ever heard of, had invaded much of Christy's body. It is believed this disease began in her liver, metastasizing into her hip, lower back, lungs, and heart.

It was known as *Hepatic Epithelioid Hemangioendothelioma (HEH).* I immediately started researching this disease and this is what I found through various sources, including medical textbooks, online medical articles, and question and answer sessions with the doctors. HEH is a rare vascular cancer which is difficult to diagnosis. There is little known about this disease, with a small amount of literature available as well. Sarcomas found in the liver as the primary source of this disease are quite unusual and more commonly affect young adults. The cause is not known, and can start anywhere in the body.

This disease affects the cells which line the inside of blood vessels. They most generally affect the soft tissues such as the liver, lungs, and bones, which in Christy's case was all true. These tumors are malignant and can go undetected, giving them time to spread to other areas quickly. It is treated with radiation and chemotherapy, but there is no specific treatment plan, as we soon came to find out.

I am sure anyone receiving this news would have been devastated, as all of us were. Christy began to cry, trying to wrap her head around the diagnosis. She looked up at her doctor and asked what her chances of survival were. He was the head of the Hematology/Oncology Department and had a great demeanor with Christy. He said with treatment it would be a long shot. She asked him if she were his daughter what he would do. He smiled and gently said he would fight, so of course, Christy smiled and told us all she wanted to do just that.

Once the team of doctors left the room and we began to sift through what we had been told, Corey and Jeff dried the tears from their eyes. I hugged my courageous daughter, and then went to the window. I remember staring at the roof of the hospital and gazing across through the windows of the other floors. There were offices with people seated at their desks, while other windows were filled with decorated Christmas trees. I had to process what we had been told and work on the words I would say to Christy.

The only thing to do was to pray for strength and courage, not only for Christy, but for all of us. At a point like this, the amount of strength you are able to pull up from deep within is hard to reach. If I had not been so deeply rooted in my faith, this news would have been hopeless. As bad as it was, my hope and trust still remained strong, and I knew that no matter what, God was with us constantly.

Christy asked for dinner from a restaurant, so Jeff and Corey left. I think she really wanted to talk with me. The first thing out of her mouth was, "I told you I was going to die of cancer before I was twenty-eight-years old." I didn't have the words to reply.

One of the saddest things I have ever witnessed was the moment I sat and listened to my daughter call her brothers and best friend to tell them she knew what was wrong and what she was about to face.

Christy called her older brother, Joshua, first to tell him what we had just learned. As quickly as he answered the phone, Christy fell apart and began to sob uncontrollably. It was the most pitiful experience to hear her gasp for air in between her words. Josh told her it would be alright and he encouraged her in such an amazing way. She stopped crying and was able to converse with him much more calmly. Josh has always been the one that keeps most of his emotions inside and generally didn't let on that his siblings were important to him. I know he always cared for them, but had to be that older brother with the attitude. Today was much different, and I hated that we were unable to all be together during such an emotional time.

Ben, Christy's little brother, was called next. He always looked up to Christy and loved to talk with her. Christy was usually the only one that could talk sense into this strong-willed child. Ben was so young when this was all playing out as he had just finished high school. He was still a bit wild and learning who he was. His big sister's words were about to tear up his world. The first thing he wanted to do was drive to Virginia when Christy broke the news to him. I felt as though my heart was being torn into pieces as I listened to these conversations.

After a few minutes, Christy called Kimmie, and that call was equally as hard for me to witness as they cried together and then laughed. Hearing my daughter utter the words, "I have cancer" cut through me deeply. Kimmie was pregnant with twin girls at this time and was going to deliver soon. She was living in Florida and could not make it to see Christy, but planned to once she was recovered from having her babies.

I wanted to talk to the doctors myself, so I went into the hall to find them, and I did. They knew I had a medical education, and I told them I wanted to hear from them the complete truth. They lowered their heads and told me that the prognosis was not at all good. They would do everything possible, but I knew what they were telling me.

Christ with a y

I knew that the only way Christy was
going to survive for any amount of time would
be to receive chemotherapy. It would be the
only thing that would shrink the existing tumors
and keep the disease from invading more parts
of her body. It had already made its way to so
many areas, and it seemed to be spreading
rapidly. A year ago, Christy was beginning her
married life and new career. She was so excited
to finally be finished with school and become a
responsible adult. Her dream of becoming a
missionary was halted as well as her strong
desire to have a baby. Life had taken a
completely different path now that was
unknown and so unwelcome to us all.

While I was talking to them, I felt a great
amount of peace sweep over me. I smiled at
them and let them know that we were ready, but

I had nothing but complete trust that we would all be guided through this next trek. I felt that I was going to take this on just like anything else and I never gave into this evil disease. I decided that we would face it head on, never letting it get the best of our attitudes. We were going to take this on with an attitude of "if" not "when".

Christy began IV antibiotics and received iron therapy once again. The doctors began discussing the treatments Christy would receive and the option of experimental treatments. They were reaching out to other hospitals that had experience with HEH, but it was so limited. We were told not to try and research this disease on the internet as there was little known about it.

We went to the bookstore so I could load up on as many books with information as possible. After our return with an array of

material, Corey went to their home in

Lynchburg to check on things and get the mail.

He always returned with tons of cards and

packages for Christy. Every other day he would

travel home, and when he came back, it was a

highlight for Christy and actually all of us to see

her smile at the thoughtfulness of so many

people.

The doctor brought in someone from

palliative care. I had never heard that term and

didn't understand it for a long time. These

doctors were to keep Christy as comfortable as

they could no matter what. There were many

things happening at this point for Christy's care.

It was now the eleventh of January and we had

been dealing with many doctors for so long

now. We were introduced to so many, we had to

write them down to keep track. Christy was in constant pain, but they were finally beginning to regulate it with medicine. For the most part, the green bean with a smile wasn't showing up as often, so that was a good sign that she wasn't receiving too much.

One night, while Christy was asleep, someone from the lab came up to draw her blood. This happened often throughout each day, and she had had enough of being poked. The technician did not wake Christy, as she would have liked, but reached for her ID bracelet to scan it before performing the blood draw. This was a mistake on his part! When Christy woke up, she turned, looked at the tech, and told him to get away from her. She firmly stated that this was not the way to take a patient's blood and gave instructions on the proper protocol. Corey was sleeping next to her, as he did every night, and told us the story the next morning. I don't believe that lab tech ever came back to draw Christy's blood. This girl may have been terribly ill, but she still had her spunk and let folks have a piece of her mind when necessary.

Christy was tiring quickly of having her blood drawn and the pain it caused. Sometimes the simple procedures in the hospital are more painful than the big ones. It was decided that Christy would receive a port in her chest near her heart for her chemo, and blood would be drawn through it as well from that point on. Christy was very nervous about getting the port inserted and beginning chemotherapy. She was really apprehensive about the first blood draw, but was assured it would be much different than the previous method. She was pleased at the ease of the procedure once it was completed.

So much was happening, including things in Michigan, for Christy. A fundraising event was planned to raise money for Corey and Christy at Texas Roadhouse by her friends. It was a great success, and so many people came to support them. Eventually, another one was held at the restaurant in Lynchburg. The outpouring of love for Christy and Corey was expressed in so many ways. The event raised a great deal of money for this sweet couple to help them pay for all the expenses that were piling up. God was good and never let them go without anything they needed. The people where Corey worked were also understanding about the time off he needed.

Christ with a y

On January 12, 2010, Christy was taken down for a radiation treatment on her hip to help her walk. The cancer was causing her a great deal of pain in this area, and the doctors all felt this would be beneficial to her. I can't explain enough how Christy's anxiety level was so high everyday. She was very afraid of every new procedure that was done to her. I began to see that Christy had lived a long time with anxiety, and it was all becoming very obvious. It was requested by Christy that Corey be with her during the treatment, but he would be exposed to radiation so it wasn't possible. Everyone could see how panicked Christy was, and they told Corey he could stay in the control room and talk to Christy through a speaker. I don't think anyone could imagine the peace this gave to Christy. This was a traumatic experience for my girl even though her husband was right there with her. The tears were once again streaming down her face as she faced yet another time of the unknown. It was bad enough that this disease was destroying her body, but the painful things that had to be done to give her a little bit of a quality life were heartbreaking.

While she was away from her room, Jeff and I began looking for wigs for Christy, knowing she would lose her hair eventually. This was a very hard thing for me to grasp. Christy always had beautiful hair, and the longest eyelashes. Here we were watching a disease take away pieces of our only daughter, and we hated it. Beauty lies within and there was so much of that in Christy. She was also physically beautiful but the disease was taking its toll on her.

I was tired, but I knew it was only the beginning of a new life for all of us—a life none of us had imagined being part of. This would be that big trial I wondered about when I was younger. As something hit this hard, there were millions of things that crossed my thoughts, but I did not question God. I was not bitter, nor did I cry out to God in any other way than to ask Him for strength and wisdom. We truly depended and continually kept Proverbs 3:5-6 in our thoughts: "Trust in the Lord with all thine heart; and lean not unto thine own understanding. In all thy ways acknowledge him, and He shall direct thy paths." Scripture was brought to our attention at the right moment throughout each day. Sometimes the familiar passages were easy to rely on. Other times verses that we were hearing differently. God was always there carrying us through the longest days of our lives.

While Jeff and Corey were out getting dinner, as they did each day, Christy and I had a nice long talk. She shared some things she had written a few years ago, and began telling me the sweetest love story I've ever heard. She told me she knew she loved Corey, but didn't realize how much until this day. During her radiation treatment, when Corey was talking through the speaker, he took her on a trip from the beginning of their relationship all the way through the present. His words were about the adventures they had shared and the plans they were looking forward to. He sang to her and put her mind at ease. He told her secrets and how much she meant to him. None of this was rehearsed, mind you, as he was hurled into this

without warning. Christy and I cried together,
the hardest we had cried through any of this.
She could hardly get through the conversation
with me without gasping for air as her feelings
were so raw.

I will always ponder this moment
because I watched something very special
occur. I witnessed a young couple being torn
apart yet meshed together. I felt a deeper love
for my son-in-law at that moment that I cannot
describe. I watched a boy become a man, and I
saw true love displayed like I have never seen. I
have watched sad love story movies that have
touched me, but nothing like this. This was real
life, and it was right in my face, piercing my
heart.

Christy received a mild dose of her
chemo at 5:00 p.m. through her port and did

well with it. It made me sad to know that this poison was going through her veins. She dealt with it like a champ. I, however, didn't deal with it well, and later that night I cried into my pillow until I couldn't cry anymore.

As if this day wasn't filled with enough, my job at the pediatrician's office was terminated. I knew they couldn't keep me on as an employee since I wasn't there, but it stung a bit. I would now take on a whole new role, and by the grace of God, I would be able to stay with my girl as long as she needed me.

~Chapter Twenty One~

January 13, 2010 was the day Christy

was released from the hospital. I was scared to

take my weak daughter home, which was an

hour and a half away. She had been in a hospital

bed for nineteen days. It was exhausting for

Christy as she rode in our pickup truck with Jeff

and me while Corey followed in their car behind

us. Just the distance from her room to the

parking structure in a wheelchair was taxing for her.

Before we left she had an orientation from the pain clinic. She began feeling the affects of the chemo and became nauseated. She slept the majority of the ride home, and getting her into the house was difficult. We took Christy directly to their bedroom where a hospital bed had been delivered for her. We made sure to get her warm and comfortable, which was not an easy task. She was so weak and tired, but we managed to get her situated. Jeff and I left to get new bedding and food, and upon our return, found Christy in her recliner in the living room. She was happy and joined us at the dinner table for tacos from her favorite fast food place, Taco Bell. It was great to see that she was able to settle in at home in such a short amount of time.

A pain medication pump was placed into Christy's port that she had to carry around. She was able to press a button when she needed relief from the constant pain. The next morning she was hitting the button quite a bit. A home care nurse was assigned to Christy, and her first visit lasted two hours. Christy became very comfortable with this nurse and was weary of anyone else touching her port. There was a great amount of trust in this nurse that I don't think I could ever explain. They bonded within minutes of her arrival. Her name was Krissie.

Great friends from where Christy worked jumped into action and did things without hesitation. Some took care of Molly, which was quite wonderful. Others bought groceries and just set them by the back door. They knew Christy was uneasy about having visitors. They made incredible dinners and offered to do many things. Some of them took me out when I needed to get away and gathered money to help pay for things. When Corey went to get Molly from the kennel, someone from the bank where Christy worked paid the bill in full. The generosity of people astounded us and it never ended.

Jeff and I went to the post office because there was a piece of certified mail for us. When we opened it, we found a check from one of his cousins. It was slightly over the amount that we had to pay for our entire hotel stay while in Charlottesville. Watching God work made us cry once again. We literally stared at each other while sitting in the car and then thanked God for caring for us.

It was decided that I would be staying with Christy and Corey for as long as I was needed. There was a bedroom and bathroom in the basement of the Oakdale house, and that is where I would set up camp. Jeff did everything to take care of me so I would be comfortable. We bought the things I would need. After, he went back home and packed all the things I requested to bring when he returned.

The next few days before Jeff went back to Michigan were spent getting things organized. Christy had so many oral medications to take, so we began working on organizing them. A new shower fixture was put in to help Christy with her showers. It was so difficult helping her shower because we had to keep the port dry. She was very concerned about it, and would become easily irritated if a drop of water was near it. We began talking about cutting Christy's hair to make it easier for her.

A few days after being home, we had to go back to Charlottesville to see the endocrinologist to regulate Christy's thyroid medication. We had decided to stay with the medical team at UVA for all of Christy's care rather than use the Lynchburg area doctors. Christy was more comfortable with this, and we wanted to make sure she was in charge of her care. Once she trusted someone, it was best to keep her under their care.

It was not easy for Christy to travel back and forth to Charlottesville as she was still weak from her long hospital stay. She was still suffering from pain, even with the high doses of medication. We made sure to keep blankets and a pillow handy for her on these trips to help her stay warm and as comfortable as possible.

Her appointment went well, but we were gone for a much longer span of time than anticipated. When we returned home, Christy was beyond exhausted. Corey and I did things quickly to get her comfortable again in the house. Of course, Molly was always thrilled to see Christy and wanted to smother her to pieces. Christy would get agitated when Molly was jumping on her, worrying the tube in her port would be yanked out. At one point, Molly's strong tail wrapped around the tubing and almost pulled the tubing right out of the port. The poor dog didn't understand, and Christy was ready to have a nervous breakdown. Corey and I jumped up from the table and kept the disaster from happening.

Corey's sister, Laurie, made it possible to get a really nice wig made for Christy from someone she knew. It didn't seem like Christy was very interested in the wigs and hair pieces we were getting for her, and I didn't understand why. I just continued to get her things I thought would make her feel pretty. We shopped at a little place in the hospital at one point for ideas of what was to come, but she literally wanted nothing to do with this visit. These experiences only made Christy upset. She continued to look to the future with a positive attitude, which was good.

The radiation treatment that Christy had been given in the hospital made a huge difference for her. She was able to get around a little easier and more comfortably. It was so sad

to watch her try to get around with the pain that

she had. She practically pulled her leg along as

she walked because it hurt her to just move it at

all. Even sitting in her chair, she would ask us to

move her leg for her.

There were always doctor's

appointments and in home care nurse visits. It

was a bit daunting trying to keep track of

everything. Additionally, the amount of

medications Christy had to take orally was

insane. We worked together planning everything

out, whether it was in Christy's planner or on a

calendar in their study. Corey had made the

extra bedroom into an office area for the two of

them, complete with built-in shelving and two

desks so they could do their school work

together. He had surprised her while she was

away visiting with us after they had moved in.

Corey was always building something and was

very good at woodwork. His job at Liberty was

making things the university needed for a

number of different areas. He helped build

beautiful pieces for the new law department the

school had just added.

~Chapter Twenty Two~

It was getting much more difficult to take care of Christy's hair, and too tiring for her to go through the ritual of combing it after a shower. We decided since we knew the chemo would begin causing the dreaded hair loss, that it should be cut. This was a day I knew was coming, and I had a difficult time accepting it.

One of Christy's friends from home had moved down to Lynchburg, and she was a hairstylist. Christy was having a very difficult time with people visiting, so this friend was the only one we could turn to for such an intimate and necessary task. I'm sure it was hard for Alicia to come and see Christy, but she was happy to have had the opportunity to do her friend's hair. Christy had become friends with Alicia when they met at church as teens. Our families were good friends, and there was a great amount of trust between us. God provided another beautiful way to give us what we needed at just the right time.

While we were at the table eating dinner prior to Alicia's visit, Christy became very weak and just put her head down on the table. She was always determined to do whatever was scheduled for her, and today was no different. She was able to get her second wind when

Christ with a Y

Alicia arrived. Christy was at ease while her friend began to work on the haircut. She put her hair into a ponytail placing a hair tie at the base of Christy's neck, and then another one at the bottom. The scissors began cutting just beneath the top of the ponytail, and twelve inches of the most beautiful hair was in my hands. Her remaining hair was cut into the Pixie Style that looked as cute as could be on Christy. About half way through, more weakness hit Christy, and she had to rest for a little bit. All the pain medication and chemo in Christy's body made it hard for her to withstand much for a lengthy period of time.

I tend to talk a lot when I'm nervous or upset, so I'm sure I was filling the moment with many words. It helped me get through what I thought would be very difficult. I'm glad that

Alicia was there and that she brought such a beautiful presence with her. She helped us all get through something I thought would have been unpleasant and sad.

I held that ponytail in my hands thinking about all that was in the future for Christy. I thought about how many times I had braided her hair, curled it, brushed it, and just simply ran my fingers through it. I thought about how much I would miss watching her throw it up in a simple ponytail or scrunch it up with some product on her way out the door. I pictured the times we fixed it in all kinds of fancy ways for cheerleading games, or how we curled it for church. I know that hair doesn't define a person, but it was a beautiful feature that Christy possessed, and it hurt me to know it would soon be gone.

Christ with a y

I asked Christy if I could keep her
ponytail, and she looked at me and just smiled.
She was grasping all of this better than I was,
but I kept it together until I went down to my
room a little later that night. Going through all
these phases of watching my daughter suffer
and accept the things that were happening to her
each day was despairing. The best word to
describe how I felt: sad. Sometimes my heart
ached, and other times I felt numb to everything
around me. The thoughts that went through my
mind would never be expressed for fear of
anyone not understanding. Pure sadness would
fill me with it lingering in my every breath. I
had to keep to myself, though, because there
were people to take care of. I felt I had a huge
responsibility to keep things going for everyone
involved.

I began to reach deeper and deeper within myself to find strength to endure everything. I was in a situation where I had no idea what each day would bring and there were so many questions—"When Christy would need something more than I could give her, or do for her, what would I do? How could I give Corey the support he needed, not really knowing how he was internalizing all of this? How could I take care of everything at home in Michigan where Jeff, Josh, and Ben were?" were all looming in my mind.

None of this was about me, but I would feel a need to just be alone I would think about what I was dealing with and how much I missed my home. I still had a son who was twenty-years-old that needed direction, my husband who was juggling a job, a home to take care of, a dog, and he was traveling almost every

weekend to Lynchburg. I missed everyone, but I

knew I was where I needed to be and fortunate

to be able to stay with Christy.

I prayed hard and often asking God to do

His will through all of this. I never let Him

leave my thoughts, and I knew that no matter

what would happen to Christy, she would be in

a situation that would glorify God. If she were

to be healed from this disease, she would show

the world more of Jesus than she already had.

But if she did not live through the battle, her life

would glorify God in so many ways. God uses

every story to glorify Him, and I held on to that

promise knowing He would see us through this

tragedy. Although the doctors had given us a

grim prognosis the day they walked into that

hospital room, each day with Christy was a beautiful gift we cherished.

We went to Charlottesville every other Wednesday for her treatments. Our first visit was on the twentieth of January. Christy made herself look cute for every appointment she went to. No matter how she felt, she would put on makeup, fix her hair, and put on clothes that were comfortable but stylish. Christy looked adorable with her new sassy haircut. She wore it well, but I wondered how long it would be before it begun to fall out. She looked pretty amazing, all things considered!

Corey dropped us off at the door of the hospital where I found a wheelchair for Christy. She could not walk very far as she was still very weak. We went upstairs to the Cancer Center where the infusion would take place and she would meet with her oncologist. We would

learn the routine as time went on, but this day

was a little scary for all three of us. We packed

snacks and books, not knowing how long we

would be there. Christy's blood was drawn

through the port, and the doctor was impressed

with her blood counts. We were excited to hear

some positive news and smiled big, easing our

minds a little bit.

The first infusion that Christy received

was a new drug called Taxotere. She was

monitored for fifteen minutes to make sure she

had no allergic reaction. She was then given anti

nausea medication, followed by her chemo,

which was called Gemcitabine. This was one of

the regiments that she would receive. Each visit

would be different as they would do one drug

alone, and then the other would be two medications combined.

Doctors from Radiology and Palliative Care came by to see how Christy was doing. We had a great team of people caring for Christy, but I feel they learned a lot from her. She was always told what an optimistic patient she was and how her smile made them feel good. Once again, that smile was impacting people and impressing them in typical Christy style.

The day was long, and traveling back to Lynchburg was exhausting for all of us. It was hard for me to stay awake in the back seat, and Christy was out cold sitting next to Corey.

Christy was still friends with people at Texas Roadhouse, the manager included. They arranged for us to pick up dinner on the way home from every chemo appointment, which was a huge help. We would call in our order and grab it on the way home from the hospital in Charlottesville. It was hard to get Christy to eat because the medications stole her appetite most days.

Everyday we would wait for the mail delivery and sort through it finding the cards just like while Christy was in the hospital. The amount of mail she would receive on a daily basis was remarkable. Gifts would arrive from friends and family from Michigan, and brighten her day. We always waited for Corey to get home from work before opening anything. That was a struggle because girls love getting things in the mail. I will admit at times, we may have opened a few prior to Corey's arrival home!

I loved how Corey came through the door each day from work. I know it was a struggle for him to stay working with his wife at home dealing with this sickness. I know he wanted to be home with her, but that was not possible. We needed him to work to pay the bills and keep the health insurance. Christy was getting short-term disability pay, but her insurance coverage came through Corey, thank the Lord!

One of my favorite parts of the day was when we would hear the backdoor open and see Molly get all excited. Corey would be putting his things down in the kitchen and yell with a cheerful voice, "Wife, how are you?" Christy would get a huge smile on her face knowing he was home, and just hearing his voice thrilled her.

~Chapter Twenty Three~

Jeff was so good about bringing things down every time he came to see us. He would pack things I had asked for, and then would make a trip to the store to bring Christy some of her favorite things that were only found in Michigan. His trips were highly anticipated, and he was so good about coming down as often as possible. We were fortunate that Jeff had an understanding boss, and told him to take whatever time he needed for his family. He never took advantage of this offer, and was able to keep up with the demands of his job as well as his life.

There were many times I would call Jeff and just burst into tears because I didn't feel like I could handle everything going on. My grandma's days were numbered as she began to have many health issues. I continued to be homesick, and I had a hard time trying to figure out my role as a caregiver. After a good cry and Jeff's tenderness, I was able to get myself back together and function better.

The weekend had finally arrived and Christy's brothers were able to come down to see her. The three of them traveled down together for a weekend visit, which made Christy happy. She missed them and wanted to see them as much as they wanted to see her. It was nice for our entire family to be together for

a few days. We weren't sure if this visit would

be the only one we would all be with each other

for.

Josh brought along his little dog, which

was great for Molly. They played together and

entertained all of us. We hung out together in

the living room, where Christy spent much of

her time. Other than sleeping in her bed at night,

she stayed nestled in her recliner. It was situated

in the corner of the living room where she could

see out the front window.

The boys and I took walks together so

we could chat and I could show them around the

neighborhood. Jeff was able to spend some time

alone with Christy, and Corey was able to get

away a little. The weekend went by much too

fast, but it was a nice couple of days spent with my kids.

The pain medication prescribed to Christy was Dilaudid, which was a very strong narcotic. It was delivered through her port, and we usually knew when it was delivering too large of a dose. She would begin to say things that made little sense and the little green bean would again appear. He showed up while the boys were there, and it made us all laugh a little bit. This was a sign that the chemo was working, lifting our spirits for a small amount of time. We would let the nurse know, and on her next visit she would adjust the dose to keep Christy from having the hallucinations.

The chemo wasn't making Christy sick like we anticipated, but it did make her tired. She slept the majority of the day, so I was on my own to do whatever I wanted to. It was too

cold to be outside, so I constantly cleaned and

rearranged things. I even ordered rugs and

curtains to spruce up the house. I took Molly for

walks and ran to the fast food restaurants some

days to mix up the day a little. I tried to get

Christy to go out with me, but most of the time

the answer was no. She would honestly try to

get the strength just to go to the store, but it was

just too draining for her. On one occasion, we

were able to go shopping for some new clothes

for her. My heart broke as I watched her trying

things in the condition she was in. It took a long

time for her to try on a pair of jeans with the

cumbersome pain pack in her way and the

weakness. She managed to try on quite a few

things, and we made some purchases, which

made her happy. Once we left the store, it was

straight home for some rest. This trip brightened my day and made my mood a little more positive for the next few days.

I wanted to get Christy out as much as possible so her muscles would stay strong but she wasn't up for it much. I did sometimes get her out to walk on the driveway a little, but she sure didn't go far. I think she was more afraid of hurting herself than she was of just getting out. She was very careful and followed all of her doctor's instructions. She moved about like someone three times her age because of the pain in her back. Her inability to breathe easily also made it hard for her to be very mobile.

One day while I was chatting with Christy, we began talking about eyelashes, and I told her the chemo would most likely affect them as well as it would her hair. She was a little upset about that and later discussed it with Corey. Again, he was able to do something so sweet as he had done while she was in the hospital. He told her, while running his fingers through her hair, which he thought she was beautiful with long hair and then found out how beautiful she looked with short hair. He then told her that he knew she would be beautiful with no hair; plus, we had a ton of "hair alternatives" for her. Christy would never use the word wig, so we came up with a different way to talk about them, and "hair alternatives" became our expressions for them. Always making her feel better was Corey's thing, and he impressed me with his ability to keep Christy's spirits lifted.

Tons of snow fell on the last day of January, and while Corey was outside shoveling it, Christy began to let her anxieties out to me. She cried many tears as she just needed to talk. Christy and I always leaned on each other because we were very close. I had written in my journal how hard it is being a young married woman, especially with cancer. We tried hard to be positive and happy but sometimes it was just hard; too hard. So when there were times to cry, we did just that and we did it together. We couldn't take the seriousness of what was happening, so in good Christy fashion, we would make fun of this disease.

As each of us played a different role in Christy's life, we all had to remember what each of us was going through as well. Cancer not only affects the patient but the people closest to them as well. I had to continually remember that Corey was a young man who was newly married and taking on so much more than any of us

could have ever imagined. He needed someone

to lean on as much as Christy needed him, and

they did well together. I did my best to be there

for them both but at the same time stay back to

allow them to be a couple. Corey also needed

his best friend, Kelsey. As close as Christy and

Kimmie were, Corey and Kelsey had a similar

friendship. When Corey and Christy began

dating, he told her how they had been great

friends for a very long time. It was really

amazing to see genuine friendship between

these two guys. I know that Corey had

explained to Christy how Kelsey was like a

brother to him, but not until Christy's illness did

she nor I realize how much their friendship

meant.

~Chapter Twenty Four~

Traveling continually to Charlottesville for appointments and treatments was taxing on all three of us. We would have to get up before the sun rose to make it on time for early arrivals at the hospital. Sometimes there were tests ordered to see if the chemo was working. Other times we saw the palliative care doctors to check to see if the pain medication was regulated correctly. There were the long days of getting tests taken, and then sitting through the chemo infusions. Christy's blood would be drawn first, and once all of her levels were checked, the drugs would be put into her port, and we would sit with her until she was finished. Sometimes this would take up to three hours. She would read or sleep, and Corey and I would sit quietly in our uncomfortable chairs supporting Christy. We always packed snacks and magazines, but we sometimes would join Christy in a nap. The trip back to Lynchburg was usually quiet because we were all tired and ready to relax in a comfortable spot at home.

It had been a month since Christy had received her first treatment, and she woke up on February fourth with tenderness on her scalp. The day had come that I was not looking forward to, the loss of her pretty hair. I helped her get ready, and as I was washing her hair, it was coming out in small clumps. I felt my heart thumping in my chest a little harder. I had been waiting for this to happen and knew it would hit me hard. It didn't seem to bother Christy until later in the day as she had the entire day to let this sink in. She began to cry, and it tore me to pieces to see her enveloped in sadness. The words from Corey soothed her and that was all she needed. A moment to let her feelings pour out, followed by another to be soothed by her prince.

I remember thinking about each day and what it would bring. In my deepest thoughts I questioned if Christy would somehow be healed. Each day had its unknowns, and my thoughts would run away all the time. I had plenty of days when my own selfishness would

come out. I wanted to stay with Corey and
Christy, but I wanted to go home in the worst
way. Life continued daily for everyone else as it
should have, but I wanted it to stop just like
mine had. Corey and Christy's lives had
changed so quickly, and to say it wasn't fair
would be wrong. Many people are affected by
illness, accidents, and death, but it was hard to
see it happening to my own flesh and blood. I
know that I am human and that I was going
through a devastating time, but I wish I had not
been thinking of myself. I should have been
more grateful that I was able to be where I was.
I was actually, exactly where I was needed, and
where God wanted me to be.

Our family had come down at the same
time Kelsey visited, and the house was buzzing
with people. This was hard on Christy as she

didn't feel good the majority of the time. They traveled through a huge snow storm and stayed at a hotel because there was not room for everyone at the house. Everyone was good about making sure to think of how Christy was feeling, but she ended up in tears knowing she had company and could not be the hostess in her own home.

As we visited with each other in the living room, all packed together just chatting, Christy began pulling out gobs of hair from her head. It was all over the floor, and she took it all in stride, sometimes even laughing. I didn't know what to do while she was doing this as it made me uncomfortable. I should have known that this would be the way Christy would handle her hair coming out. I believe she figured there was no use crying about what she couldn't control, so she decided to just roll with it.

The visit was short and when my parents, sister, nieces, and brother-in-law were ready to leave, I remember falling apart. It was so hard to see everyone walking out the door and saying goodbye. When Christy saw me crying she began to sob, and it was a total meltdown. I tried to explain why I was so sad, but it only made Christy feel worse because she was feeling bad for me. Corey took Christy to their room to console her, and Kelsey and I sat and talked for a bit. It was nice for me to talk with him as we learned things from each other about how Corey was dealing with everything.

Four days after the thinning hair, Christy had had enough and pulled out the shaving equipment. She came downstairs to my room to get me and began removing the remaining hair she had. She laughed the entire time, and I didn't know whether to laugh or cry. She was so funny that I chose to laugh with her. She shaved as much as she could reach, and then handed me the shaver. I hated each stroke but did as she asked. She then bathed, put on makeup, and adorned her earlobes with earrings. She put on a sassy hat along with a cute outfit, and much to my amazement, looked beautiful. We even took a little car ride to grab some lunch together. I loved these moments when I had my girl with me smiling and laughing.

Once again, a test was ordered for Christy that she was fearful about having done. It was an MRI that she dreaded, as she wasn't sure she would be able to handle it. We tried to get an order for an open MRI but couldn't make

that happen. The procedure was later in the day
and took a long time for everything to get lined
up. Once they were ready for her, she was given
some medication to calm her, and she did well.
When she was finished, we took her out for
dinner, which was always a big deal. When she
was hungry for something, there was a small
window of opportunity to get it to her. She
could only take small amounts of time on her
feet, so we had to act quickly.

We accomplished what had to be done,
and made our way back to Lynchburg to get
Christy back into her comfortable spot. As we
pulled into the driveway, she began to get very
cold, which was unusual, and it took us quite a
bit of time to get her into the house. It was
getting late and Christy was very emotional, so

we did a lot of talking to her helping alleviate whatever she was experiencing.

Jeff had been traveling all day to spend the weekend with us and arrived within minutes of Corey and I calming Christy. He walked into her room with a giant blue and white stuffed bear along with a bag of goodies that Christy loved. It was good to see her smile and the comfort that her dad had given her after a long day was much needed. She was finally warm and comfortable, falling asleep knowing the MRI was behind her.

During Christy's freshman year at Liberty, she met a girl named Susan who she loved, and they had become very good friends throughout the years. Susan was married and had a family whom Christy adored. Christy traveled to Virginia Beach to visit her sweet family. Susan was given the ability to display tremendous love for others. On many occasions, Susan tried to visit Christy in the hospital, but as mentioned, Christy wanted to see no one. She was just too ill to handle being around anyone. I know this hurt Susan, and it hurt us terribly to not allow her to come up to be with her friend, but we had to respect Christy's wishes.

It was close to Valentine's Day and Susan had packed a box full of things for this holiday. Her box included everything to set a romantic table for Corey and Christy, complete with tablecloth, confetti, and decorations. She had all kinds of cards and presents, too!

Corey and I went shopping for a gift for Christy the day before Valentine's Day. It was really the first time we had been together without Christy or Jeff, so we began to have a very honest and sincere conversation. Corey confided in me what was going through his thoughts and the dreams that he had for Christy and him. We talked very frankly about Christy's illness, which we hadn't done. He was having a more difficult time with all of this than I had realized. He was thrown into something so big, so awful, and so unexpected. How grateful I was for this conversation as I again began to see Corey in a different way. I was seeing things in him I would have most likely never knew existed. He was really such a very, young adult, but turning into a responsible man. I am certain that he thought it wasn't possible to be learning a lifetime of lessons in such a short amount of time. He loved Christy the moment they met, and that love had grown so much. Corey had a difficult time understanding how this could be his life. He promised to care for his wife through sickness, but that day was to come much later in their lives. Corey was so honest with his feelings sharing his heartache with me. His inability of being able to fathom the unexplainable things he was facing.

Devotionals are filled with stories of hope, faith, and miracles, but I always read them about other people. When you're put into a situation you didn't sign up for, it changes things quickly. Faith is stirred and you have to dig deeply to make sure your trust is put into high gear. I realized how much trust I had and how my faith was being used. Keeping me from sinking was a constant battle, but I had to keep Christy uplifted and Corey well grounded. I had to stay strong and God gave me the amount of strength I needed to get through not only each day, but each situation that arose.

I also began to see my husband in a completely different way as he was torn into many roles. He was taking care of everything at home while doing his forty-hour-per-week job. He was making sure the dog was groomed and the house was clean, as he knew it would ease my worries. Jeff made sure that Josh and Ben were okay and took care of the bills. When he would make the trek down almost every weekend, he made sure to bring Christy and me gifts. Jeff would take me shopping, which was a struggle for him, and take me to nice dinners. This was good for everyone involved, as it gave us all time away from each other and time alone with our spouses.

Christ with a y

On Sundays, Jeff and I would go to
church at Thomas Road Baptist Church, and
sometimes cry when a song was sung. Some of
the music played would remind us of Christy's
days at Liberty, while others would just reassure
us with the words that God was choosing for us.
There was something very special about
attending church services at this place of
worship, and I'm glad we were able to go.

Alicia was still coming over to help with
all the hair needs. She cut Corey's hair and
trimmed up all of Christy's hair essentials in
case she decided to wear them one day. I have a
special place in my heart for Alicia. She was
always so strong when she visited, and I know it
was not easy for her to see her friend suffering. I
know she detected in my face the sadness I was
experiencing, but she never let on. Alicia and

Christy's friendship was bonded together forever during these days, and I would build on that friendship in the future.

I began to understand Christy's desire to only wear hats and scarves on her hairless head. She felt it was as if she were giving into the idea that she had cancer. It was the way she dealt with it, although knowing in her heart she had this terrible illness. Once when Alicia came over to work on the hair pieces, Christy was overwhelmed with grief, and she began once again to cry. It was decided to put them all away in a box and not mention them anymore.

God knew the friends I needed and sent them to me in some fascinating ways. Our church high school group came down to Liberty to check out the campus. Every few months, Liberty has an event for prospective students entitled "College for a Weekend". Each year our church would bring the youth group down for this event, and this was the way Christy found that God was leading her to Liberty. It was so good to see some of our church family. They invited me to meet them for dinner twice while they were there. We made a little video of everyone sending well wishes to Christy since she wanted no visitors. God sent me a new friend during this weekend, Lisa, and we have remained great friends since that day. It has always amazed me how these visits from family and friends helped me so much.

We thought it might be a good idea to try and feed Christy organic foods, so we started looking through special cookbooks. We were willing to try whatever we could to help our girl. We were given a juicer and began trying to do that along with our all natural foods. We had

some interesting experiences with our recipes

for the juicer and had some great laughs. A

certain young man threw in a little too much

ginger in on one occasion and almost made us

all sick. We shared a bit of laughter after that

mistake and never used ginger in our recipes

again!

The prayer I prayed so often was that

Christy wouldn't have to be hospitalized with

setbacks. I was praying that she wouldn't have

to spend days in the hospital because her disease

was causing vital organs to have issues. I didn't

want to see her dwindle or have to make

difficult decisions about life support. Whenever

she would have issues, I would pray that they

wouldn't turn into more suffering for Christy.

God was so faithful to that request as he kept

her from any of those issues throughout the

illness.

~Chapter Twenty Five~

Molly! Oh, Molly! At times I was so
upset dealing with this large yellow lab. She
was still a puppy at heart, although she was two
years old and weighed a ton. She wanted to get
in my lap all the time, and if I didn't do what
Molly wanted she would stare at me and bark
nonstop. It was a bark that gave me a headache,
and at times I wanted to lose my mind. I loved
taking her for walks, but she was the one in

control of where we went, and sometimes that was pulling me down to the ground! On one of our walks through the neighborhood, she took me to my knees as she was so excited to meet a bulldog on the sidewalk named Luis. I was so embarrassed falling down in front of total strangers right into a nice puddle of wet mud. They were so sweet asking me if I was alright, and as I walked away with a red face I could hear the two ladies laughing. In my mind I could just hear them whispering through their giggles, "Bless her heart!" The southern way of verbalizing, "I'm glad that wasn't me eating the pavement."

On top of these special moments of dog walks and barks, this dog never stopped shedding. I would clean the hardwood floors, only to start all over again once I finished. Her hair would weave its way through the fabric of clothing, furniture, and throw rugs. She was still eating things off the counter and stealing plastic ware from the kitchen sink. She would run away as fast as she could to chew up and devour all of her findings. If her tail wagged anywhere near you, it was like getting beat with a whip. She was a happy dog, and I know she sensed that her favorite girl in the world was not herself. I could tell she missed Christy's attention. I was glad we had her, though, because dogs can make you feel better on your worst day. Molly was my therapist some days: bringing her down to my room, cuddling with her, and talk. She usually listened, but more times than not, talked back because she had more to say than I did.

We had many invitations for play dates with other dogs for Molly, but Christy wanted her right at home with her, probably for a sense

of security. The two most wonderful people, Liz

and Caroline, Christy had befriended from

work, were always there to help out. They took

care of Molly while we were away for the long

visits to the hospital. The compassion they had

for Christy was pretty amazing and we were

always grateful for their kindness. They made

special dinners, delivered groceries, took me out

to eat on several occasions, and just genuinely

did whatever was necessary to ease some stress.

Liz and Caroline had only been friends

with Christy for a short time. None of them

were actually from Lynchburg, but were

transplants from other states. The three of them

were completely different individuals, but had

woven together a unique friendship. There was

always laughter wherever they were, which is

always the best medicine. Although, Christy

kept her friends at a distance while she was ill,

Liz and Caroline knew how to send messages or

packages to the house to brighten her days.

~Chapter Twenty Six~

As the dreary winter months were turning into hints of spring, the sun began to shine more. There were still occasional days when it snowed and the roads would get icy. On those days, I would stay put in the house and read or wait for Christy to need me. She was able to get herself ready for each day very slowly, and I would just do whatever she asked of me. Sometimes she would be up early and try

to surprise me by making her own breakfast.
These were sweet moments that made me smile
and see how hard Christy was trying to take care
of her own needs.

As always, Christy meticulously kept a
calendar with all of her upcoming appointments.
Each doctor's appointment, treatment, and nurse
visits were written on the appropriate date,
making sure Corey and I knew how to plan for
each day. She made sure that her home care
nurse appointments were scheduled, and that the
medications she needed were available and
organized for all visits.

We received boxes of needles, batteries,
and bags of pain medication weekly. Krissie
would change the medication bag, and it was
my job to make sure everything was readily
available to her at each of her visits. This meant

making sure Molly was in her crate as well so

she wouldn't interfere with the care Christy

would receive. She was just too friendly with

the visitors, and it made Christy uptight. I was

taught how to change the medication, but

Christy was more comfortable with Krissie. My

medical training was such a blessing through

this ordeal as I was able to understand so much

of what was happening. I was able to do more

than just be a bystander and assist a little when

needed.

    After the nurse visits, Christy would be

exhausted because they were early in the

morning. It was very hard for Christy to get

going at the start of each new day. She always

made sure she was bathed and had some

makeup on her face. She would wear her

favorite little brown hat to cover her bare head. I

liked it when she wore her hats because it was still hard for me to see her without her hair.

There were many days when Christy would only be out of bed for a few hours. She had different symptoms on different days that were hard for her to deal with. Sometimes the area that was most painful for her was in her upper abdomen. The lesions on her liver would cause her great discomfort. Sometimes she would complain about how every bone in her body ached. Other days it would be her hip. The nausea would sometimes arise, but the medication usually helped with that. Then there were the days she had horrible headaches. Thankfully, they were nothing that we couldn't control ourselves with over-the-counter medications. Christy was fighting as hard as she could and trying to stay optimistic, but she

would get knocked down easily with the pain
and inability to just be joyful.

Although we each had an important role
in running the household, it was confusing at
times. Christy was the priority, of course, and
she could call the shots on most things. There
was the usual upkeep of things around the house
as well as fixing things that had broken. I was
the mom and mother-in-law who did whatever
necessary to make sure everything was in place
and to keep Christy happy and comfortable. I
tried to make sure I didn't interfere with their
relationship and how they managed their home.

We all really did a good job working
together, but it was not always easy. There were
days when we all wanted to say how we really
felt, but the only one allowed to do that was
Christy. Feelings were sometimes hurt, and that

was okay because we all loved each other and treated each incident that arose with respect towards one another. Within days of the hurt feelings, Christy and I would always talk out the issues and resolve them. I was beginning to get more and more homesick all the time because I had no idea what each day held or how long I would be away from my normal life. Normal would be something that would never be the same again, and I pondered on that thought as each day passed.

I turned forty-eight years old in the midst of everything, and on top of Christy's illness, my grandma was beginning to decline rapidly now. At ninety-four, she needed to live with my parents, and this was difficult on my mom as she had a rough time dealing with sickness. With her granddaughter so ill, her daughter away, and her mother failing, I knew this was a lot for her to handle. I couldn't be home to help her, and she couldn't be with us in Virginia. My individual relationships with my grandmother, mom, and daughter have been the best. They are very strong women and have taught me many things throughout my life. The bond between us has been a blessing from God, and we have loved each other deeply. I really wanted to be with my grandma during her last days, but it was not possible.

It was mid March, and we were able to get out for a bit, which was always good for the two of us. The trips were never very long, and most of the time Christy remained in the car while I ran errands. That was okay because for a short period of time I was hanging out with my best friend, the girl who sang in crazy voices.

She had something funny to say about everything. The silly girl who had popped CD's into the car radio, repeating Mandarin Chinese words to make me laugh. She had tried to learn the difficult language before she had gone to China. Her head would bob while speaking each syllable of what she had learned. She was simply the one I had so much fun with on a regular basis. The Jesus loving Child of God that witnessed to homeless people before giving them a gift card and introducing herself in a way no one else could do. Here I was, driving around the college town where she left her mark, and I loved each tiny minute of it.

Our favorite places to get food were Subway, Taco Bell, and Jersey Mike's. Walking into some of these places, Christy was instantly recognized, and they would have her food ready before ordering. We weren't really fast food junkies, but this happened because of the impact my girl had on people so easily. She was real, and she was thoughtful, and people could see something special in her. Christy would become your friend in a matter of minutes, and she never had to say a word to find out she was Christ-like.

It was decided that I needed to go home to ease my homesickness, and I would be gone for five days. I had things to take care of, and it would be a quick little break. It was hard to make plans because each day the symptoms were different for Christy. Whenever the treatments were working, the pain medication would need adjusting because that little old green bean would show up. As the days were nearing for me to leave, Christy had acute pain

in her side again. It was the worst it had been
since coming home from the hospital stay. After
a short while, we were able to help her through
the pain and, she was much better. I was
grateful once again to be able to control things
without a visit to the emergency department.

On the seventeenth of March, we went to
the hospital for Christy's regular appointment.
She was to have a CAT scan and chemo
infusion that morning. We woke up at 5:30 a.m.
to travel to Charlottesville as always. The scan
showed neither new growth nor any new
shrinkage of the tumors. The oncologist said
that Christy was very tough, and he was always
impressed with her. I know deep down he didn't
think Christy would be where she was at this
point. Her blood work was good, and the other
tests were better than expected. God was

definitely in this with us, and I know the doctors could see that.

Christy had greater difficulty with her anxiety now, and who wouldn't? Dealing with all that she was would drive anyone to feel this way. Even as sick as she was, she still held on to the thought of going back to work in a few weeks. My daughter was very driven, and cancer wasn't going to stop her! The palliative care doctor was wonderful, and she finally broke through to Christy that it would be alright to take some anti-anxiety medication. Thankfully, Christy agreed. A prescription was ordered for Christy, but she was still apprehensive about taking medication for something she thought she could control. She told me it felt like she was giving in. She was feeling as if she were not being strong enough, so we continued to let her know it was alright to need help. She accepted our words reluctantly, and made the decision to get a prescription.

After leaving this appointment and getting some lunch, my phone rang; it was a call from my mom informing me that my grandma had passed away. I was sad but relieved for my grandma as we all knew where she was now. No more suffering, no more pain, as she was in the arms of Jesus!

It was decided that I would leave the next day to be at the funeral. This would extend my stay at home a few more days and then I would return to Virginia on the date that was previously scheduled to take my original trip home. Christy was very emotional about me being gone and cried when I left. We were thankful for the new medication because it helped her once she took it. I was so torn about leaving because, although I wanted to go home, I was feeling guilty about leaving Christy. Everything was a tug-of-war with emotions at this time, but I knew I needed to be away for a short period.

While I was away, Corey made arrangements for his sister to come down to stay with Christy to care for her. It gave him peace of mind while he was at work to know Christy had someone there with her. Laurie was good medicine for Christy. She was someone she loved, and I think it perked her up in many ways. It was a good time for me to be away and for her to have someone different to talk to. I was grateful for Laurie's visit and what she did for Christy's morale!

The funeral was more of a celebration of my grandma's life, and I know Christy wished she could have been there, but, given her condition, it was impossible for her to travel. I was honored to give the eulogy for her, as I did my paternal grandmother's funeral a few years prior. I shared the stories of how fun she was when we all got together. All of my cousins were girls, so we shared the same memories. The message of salvation was given so people would know that if they knew Jesus, they would see this wonderful person again one day, and if they didn't know Him, how they could.

I spent my time at home doing regular things with the people I loved. I spent time with Buddy and my family, met with friends, and went to church. I cleaned the house from floor to ceiling because that's what I like to do, and just enjoyed being with my husband and boys. I talked to Christy constantly and missed one chemo infusion appointment while being gone. It was strange to not be with her for this; I hadn't missed a chemo treatment yet, and enjoyed playing the role of support buddy for my daughter.

When I arrived back in Virginia, it was now spring, and we were able to spend time outside. I was only back for a few days before Jeff came down for his usual visit. What a committed husband and father he was all this time, making sure to visit his favorite girls. He traveled a different route on occasion to mix things up a bit. We never knew what he was going to bring us, but he always brought something to put a smile on Christy's face.

I was happy to be back with Christy and felt refreshed to do what was needed. She was still having trouble eating because her appetite was just gone most of the time from medication. Her immune system was weak, easily contracting viruses like the common cold. It was hard to believe since we rarely left the house! She got through each illness, fortunately.

Christy looked at her calendar and canceled her regular dentist appointment. She had a difficult time canceling it because she always did the things she was supposed to do. Before making the phone call, she asked me if I thought she should schedule one for six months later. I told her she should just wait, and her reply was that she may not even be here for it anyway. That moment was one that took my breath away, and I felt a stab at my heart.

Hearing my daughter say those words was horrible, but a reality check. All I could respond with was that we never know what our future holds; only God knows our scheduled day of being taken home. It was hard to stay on top of my game at times. I never wanted to say anything that would indicate to her that she might not make it. We had no idea how long she was going to live, and my quick responses were important. Sometimes they made her laugh, and other times they sent her into a tear fest.

Kelsey's mom decided it would be nice to write a memory book for Christy and sent her a small tape recorder and journal. She sent her a sheet of questions to help her with the process. The questions were simple, asking what her favorite things were and what some of her good memories from childhood were. It sat for a long time before Christy had the strength to get it started, but once she did, she enjoyed it. I was glad she began working on this project, as I knew her recordings would be treasured in the future.

Easter Sunday arrived, and Jeff took me to church at Thomas Road. It was nice to visit this place, and I loved the music that was sung. We made it a habit to attend church whenever we were in Lynchburg. Emotions ran high being there while Christy was sick, as so many things that were said kind of squished our hearts. It was a constant battle keeping the tears welled up inside. Breathing deeply became a way to hold them back because we didn't want to have others asking us what was wrong. We couldn't talk to others about what we were experiencing because the pain was too much for us to express.

I wanted to melt into Jeff's arms many times, but that was an immediate downfall for me because I would fall into a million pieces. He knew when to hold me and when to just smile, which I was grateful for. Jeff had such a beautiful way of consoling me and he was able to do the same for Christy.

It always scared me when Christy's pain would cause issues because I didn't know how to help her. One day she had pain in her chest, and I didn't know if the tumor in her heart was growing or just causing discomfort. The only thing I could do for her was to just be there and talk her through the moments. Jeff would usually have to walk away because it hurt him too much to see his girl in pain. He was the guy that took charge in most cases, but his sensitive side would overpower him when it came to seeing Christy suffer. The pain subsided

eventually, and she was able to rest comfortably

once again.

~Chapter Twenty Seven~

The gentle breezes of spring were welcoming the month of April, and there were signs that Christy was feeling worse each day. There were now days she remained in her bed, and times she wouldn't eat anything. She tried hard every day to challenge herself and make the days as normal as she could, pulling all the energy she had to even smile. We tried to take her out, but she wasn't able to. She cried often and her body ached with pain. When the nurse came to change the needle in her port now, Christy would cry because it hurt, and she was just finished with all of this. Corey and I could see how discouraged she was becoming.

We were on the fifth round of chemo treatments and Christy faired well with them. Other than the nausea becoming more common she was still dealing with the side effects well. We met with the oncologist, who seemed to be getting quite comfortable with us. He liked to talk to Christy, but then again, who didn't?

On this particular day getting ready to drive up to UVA, I had an idea. I had bought two dresses accidently. They were the same size but different colors. I asked Christy if she'd like to wear one of them, and she chose the one in black. It was just a simple cotton sundress perfect for the warm April weather. She found a black hat, black flip flops, and a cute bracelet to accessorize the outfit. It was so nice to see my girl all fancy and pretty. I think it made her feel better to be all dressed up. She flashed those baby blue eyes with a little violet eye shadow and out the door we went.

As we sat for hours and hours at the hospital, I would begin to let my thoughts wander, which was sometimes dangerous, other times therapeutic. I began to look back on how I cared for my children. I did what I always thought was best for them and wanted them to grow up healthy. I wondered if it was something I had done to cause Christy to become filled with this dreaded disease. I honestly think that she had been sick far longer than anyone had realized. I thought about the time spent trying to figure out why she had always been nauseated in the mornings and couldn't eat breakfast. She was always able to make this horrific grinding noise with her right hip, and her lower back always hurt. She was never diagnosed with asthma, but had asthmatic symptoms. Christy tired much quicker than the girls her age, but had a driving force in her to always stay on top of her game. The only place in her body where the cancer had not shown symptoms prior to her diagnosis was the in her heart. Although physically there was an issue there, that heart was incredibly strong. Christy's heart was giving and pure, never finding bad in anyone or anything. When I saw that tumor in the pictures they had taken, it crushed me. The plan was to eventually remove that tumor, but it was an extremely risky surgery. Christy was taking blood thinners to make sure the tumor didn't keep the blood from flowing through the chambers incorrectly.

On May 15, 2010, Corey was set to graduate with his Masters Degree from Liberty. We were beginning to plan this big event, and it was filling Christy with immense worry. We had to plan for the out of town family that was coming to participate in the celebration. Corey and Christy were still working on putting their married lives together, so their house wasn't set up quite yet for guests. We had to find places for people to sleep, and there was a shortage of space. Christy liked things thoroughly organized and wanted everything to be impeccable. This was the girl who planned an entire prom while she was in high school, so she knew what to do. This was a bit of a struggle now that the recliner in the living room was where most of her time was spent.

We should have been more insistent to Christy that the guests would have to stay in a hotel but we were dealing with a woman with leadership skills. I could see how overwrought this was making Christy, but we still had another month. We tried to just minimize it as much as possible.

There were still the occasional days that Christy did well. Sometimes I would leave for several hours on the weekends so Corey and Christy could have time together. I knew it was important for them to have a chance to be two loving people sharing their thoughts and dreams. I'm sure there were things they wanted to say to one another but kept them inside for fear of discussing the unknowns of the future.

On the good days, or even just the good hours, Christy and I would have long conversations about so many things. I admired her character. She was so caring, and I was always amazed at how God had designed her. I was blessed to have been given a child like her. Her younger years were spent searching for answers as to how God could love her so much. Christy prayed for people relentlessly and always put the needs of others above her own. I know she helped many of her friends with their problems and invested in them wholeheartedly. Christy gave herself to people, and I believe that is more precious than any physical gift anyone could ever receive. She never expected anything in return, nor did she look for praise. I believe that Christy was extremely humble the way she lived and kept many things between herself and God.

One afternoon we spent hours outside on our chaise lounges talking about anything and everything. We were still able to laugh and cry about life. On this particular day, I asked Christy if she had ever thought about what she would want if something were to happen to her. I knew this was a very touchy subject, but I needed to know her thoughts. The look she gave me was intense, and I knew the question that would follow. Asking this would make her think I thought she wouldn't make it through this. I was beginning to wonder if she would, but we never used the word "if." I wanted to know what she wanted to do and told her I was only asking because I had written out my wishes. I explained to her that she should write it all out, seal it in an envelope, and give it to me. We do

not know the number of days God has given to

us, so we need to be ready for his call home. We

never know when we will take our last breath,

and I just wanted Christy to tell me her thoughts

so I could carry them out the way she would

want. I also knew that she would have specific

things she loved and wanted the world to know

about. She began asking me what my wishes for

myself were, and I shared them with her very

delicately. She soaked in what I had told her,

and I knew she was meditating on my words.

Christy rarely came down to the

basement where my room was due to the

difficulty she experienced with moving up and

down stairs. Later that evening after our

conversation, she made her way down to hand

me a sealed envelope that simply said "my

wishes." I knew what it was and what a crushing feeling to be handed that envelope, but it was what I had requested. I put it in my suitcase and hoped to never have to be the one to open it. She spent a few minutes with me, not mentioning anything about the envelope, and went back to her chair in the living room.

~Chapter Twenty Eight~

On April 14th, we headed to UVA for
more chemo, and the weather was beautiful. The
tree that attracted Christy to their house was in
full bloom. It was filled with pretty, pale pink
flowers, and the ground below was littered with
petals that had found their way to break free
from the limbs. It was the sign of new life
beginning as the days were warming in the
mountains of Virginia. The sky was blue with

just a few drifting clouds, which made it a perfect day to capture a few pictures. The previous owners left a little cement bench under the tree, and with quite a long convincing conversation with Christy, I was able to capture one of the most breathtaking photos of her.

Christy was dressed and ready to head up to the hospital for her treatment, so I knew I had a very small window of opportunity to take the pictures. Christy did not want photos of herself because she said if she made it through her disease; she did not want anyone to see her like that. If she did not make it through, she wanted people to remember her how she was when she was healthy. I knew she would not want me to share the images I caught that day, so I never shared them, they remained only for me to cherish.

Christ with a Y

My equipment was not digital so I had to wait for the images to be developed. I knew they would be beautiful. The way the morning light was laying across the canvas was ideal for obtaining just how beautiful my girl was. Christy was as pretty as the flowers that were blooming above her. I was looking forward to seeing what the camera had caught.

The infusion was much more painful this time around, which was not easy for Christy. Accessing her port was causing her great discomfort, and the tears silently fell from her face. Corey touched her arm to comfort her, and she cried all the more as the pain was now spreading throughout her entire body. With Christy's strong dislike of being touched, it was sometimes perplexing to find ways to soothe her in times like these. It was agonizing for Corey and me to watch her suffer so intensely.

We made it back to the house late that evening, and Caroline was waiting for us with dinner. She made the best food, and we were enthusiastically waiting to see what she had prepared. As we entered the neighborhood close to home, there was a terrible smell coming from a car. It was burning oil, and it somehow made Christy very sick. We barely made it home and had to whisk her into the house right past Caroline. I felt so bad doing this because she was so happy to see us, but she also understood the situation.

We helped Christy get into comfortable clothes, and got her into bed as she shivered and cried. The treatments were beginning to drastically take their toll on her.

Christ with a Y

At the appointment earlier, there was a woman around Christy's age receiving her treatment, and she looked very ill. Christy zoned in on her and mentioned her appearance. I tried to change the subject, but she remained in Christy's thoughts. She continued to talk about her as she continued to cry. She told me how she could feel the chemo going through her veins and how looking at the girl scared her. It was a difficult day for all of us. I sat and held her hand trying to comfort her the best way I could, and within a few minutes, she looked at me and asked me why I was holding her hand. This was just how Christy was. She was able to quickly calm herself in unique ways. Once again, these moments made me smile and laugh even in the midst of depressing moments. Corey brought us each a piece of magical cake from

Caroline with a grin on his face, and we all felt better. Dessert is always better before dinner!

Things were beginning to change a bit, and I was feeling unsettled. I would call Jeff every evening, and he was feeling it as well. All we knew to say was how despicable this whole situation was for all of us. We were individually dealing with our emotions and trying to live each day with hope, but the days were now becoming more difficult.

When Christy received the email on April 6th that her position was no longer waiting for her, it hit her hard. She had worked so diligently for her degree and wanted to continue working her way up at the bank. Her responsibility as a wealth management associate made her feel important. She was asking constantly to receive more training so she could

advance. She was a great employee and worked
even when she could hardly make it into the
office. Christy was great friends with the people
she worked with including her bosses. On many
occasions, she was asked to house sit, pet sit,
and babysit for her co-workers. She was trusted
by many, and she was happy to help her friends.

I saw Christy cry when she received the
email. I knew how badly it hurt her. She had
been working since she was old enough to
babysit. She placed a high priority on being the
best employee possible wherever she worked,
and, although deep down she knew she could no
longer work, it stung.

I truly melted everyday watching
Christy's life change so dramatically. During
her childhood, I could only help guide her into
the person the Lord wanted her to become—

always standing by as her sideline cheerleader. I

knew she would strive to be the best at

everything she did, and if she failed at

something, it would only set her on a course for

something bigger and better. I was so excited

for her when she achieved her ambitions. The

excitement I felt was as if it were my own

dreams coming true. Even though she excelled,

she was always hesitant about moving forward.

Her prayer life was outstanding, and she put her

faith and trust in God's hands. I was recurrently

awestruck with the courage she found in Christ.

Although her life at this point was so opposite

of where we thought it be, Christy was always

brave and faithful to her Heavenly Father.

As the middle of April approached,

Christy's symptoms were constantly changing

from one day to the next. The pain was different

and the tears came more frequent. Trying to

comfort her as she had gone through so much

day in and day out for so many months was

exasperating, and finding the right words was

nearly impossible. The hair follicles on her head

were even causing her much pain. Each breath

was now more and more difficult for her. I

trusted that God knew the limit of what I could

handle. All the obvious things I prayed about

during this time, but it was a little prayer I

barely spoke that was so graciously answered.

The prayer I seemed to only whisper to Him: to

not let Christy suffer and waste away before my

eyes. The word onto which I held was hope.

What would we have done without the God of

the Universe watching over us and knowing that

He would get us through this awful season of

suffering? It was pure anguish watching Christy

go through a disease that was gravitating

through her body at a much faster rate now. It

was a mental suffering as well as the physical

for her. For those who loved her, it was a

torturous event not knowing how long she

would live. The feeling of numbness and the

exhaustion that overwhelmingly took the place

of joy and happiness was becoming a part of

each day. The only thing to do was to gravitate

towards our Lord because He was who would

give us everything we needed.

Life continued to go on for everyone, but

our lives were stuck. My heart ached every

moment for Christy. As a parent, watching tears

fall from my daughter's face almost daily was

an indescribable feeling. She tried to live

normally by keeping her calendar and trying to

be the wife she wanted to be. I watched Corey

and Christy strive to complete the task of each day, but the sickness made it emotionally draining.

Headaches were bothering Christy now to the point of it feeling as though she had been hit with a baseball bat. She had trouble expressing her thoughts verbally, and there were sores appearing in her mouth. Oh, how I hated the suffering and not being able to do anything for her. While dealing with each new issue, she never looked for pity. She just would muster the strength to endure and move past the episodes that plagued her body.

Christy knew I was preparing to go home for a few days again, and I knew that God was giving her the strength to be away from me during that time. The day before I left, she was strangely feeling better. There were many mother-daughter moments I will always cherish, and the times I was able to help Christy with the routines of getting ready for the day were my favorite. She would let me help her get dressed and help her put on makeup. We would often giggle and joke about how we should fix her cute bald head, which was just filled with fuzz now. I always loved dolling Christy up when she was little. On her wedding day, we broke away from the wedding party and went into her bedroom to apply her makeup. That was one of my favorite days, but every day I was able to spend with my girl was a huge blessing.

I spent the weekend at home just being with my family. I was so torn, once again, about being home away from Christy. It felt wonderful to be there but my heart was still in Virginia on Oakdale Drive. I had given Jeff concert tickets to see Carrie Underwood for Christmas, and this was a quick trip home for me to relieve my homesickness that was ever present. We listened to the music she sang, and we both became overwrought with emotion. Music is always what brings tenderness to my heart, and her songs will always take us back to that time in our lives when everything stood still.

I arrived back in Lynchburg the evening of April 27th, and Christy met me with a big hug. She had cleaned out closets and had been very active while I was away. It was so strange to see her like that since the week prior had been so dramatically different. Again, God's grace was given to us at a time we needed some!

Jeff and I would be celebrating our twenty eighth wedding anniversary together in Virginia. We have never been able to do one of the anniversary getaways. There was always something going on while our kids were growing up. Our twenty-fifth anniversary was the same year Corey and Christy were married, so all of our funds went into the expenses of their wedding. We did not mind that a bit because that was such a special year. We have never been big on the extravagant things in life because we enjoy the more simplistic side of life. We have been given all we need to be happy. Jeff and I had a nice dinner at our favorite restaurant nearby and spent the rest of our time with Christy and Corey.

Before leaving to go back home, Jeff and I attended church in the morning. The message was from 1 Kings 19, and it was like God purposely prepared this message for Rev. Jonathan Falwell to deliver to my heart. This story about Elijah said he was afraid for his life,

so he sat under a bush and prayed that he might

die. He told the Lord he had had enough and fell

asleep under the bush. After instruction from an

angel, the Lord appeared before Elijah and

questioned him. What caught my attention in

this message was that a powerful wind shattered

the rocks of the mountains, but the Lord was not

in the wind. There was an earthquake but the

Lord was not in the earthquake. A fire came, but

the Lord was not in the fire either. In a gentle

whisper, Elijah heard God's voice. I thought

about the journey we were on, and this was such

a beautiful description of how God was working

in me. He was gently whispering to me all the

time that He would be with us every moment,

never leaving us in our present storm.

Corey and I went to get some ice cream later that evening, and we began to talk. He let his feelings out and was reminiscing about the days while he was dating Christy. He started telling about one of the early dates when he had asked her the question about her upbringing. She told him it was great, and that she would not change a thing. Corey said he fell in love with her at that moment. I realized how special Corey was and that I would always want him to be part of our family. Christy patiently waited for the man that God sent to her, and she was very wise to do that. So often we are impatient and we grab the first thing that comes our way with great impatience. I found this so intriguing about Christy's personality. She prayed and waited for God's answers for His plan for her. There were many emotional stages Christy had gone through in her young life, but she held strong to the promises she knew God would keep, and He never left her prayers unanswered. I do not remember her ever asking why she had gotten sick but trusting that this trail would glorify God in some way.

Christy was finished with her regiment of chemo treatments, and we were waiting to go to her appointment on May 5th to have a CT scan with contrast to see what was next. The tumor in her heart had remained the same, and getting around was more difficult for my girl. Her hip and back were giving her constant pain, and she was limping again. She had to pick up her leg to move it because of the pain, just as it had been when we first came home from the long hospital stay in January. Her left shoulder was beginning to give her trouble, and the area in her side was making her uncomfortable.

Since Jeff had left, Christy was hardly getting

out of bed and slept the majority of the time

now. If I went to check on her, she would open

her eyes and smile at me, asking me to just let

her sleep.

The days leading up to Christy's next

appointment in Charlottesville, on the fifth of

May, began to feel heavy. We had no clue what

to expect or what was next. Christy was always

so anxiety ridden for her appointments and had

medication to help her through them. She took

the prescribed medication the night before our

travels to UVA.

An early arrival for the scan was first on

the list of appointments, and then a visit with the

oncologist. She still had eyelashes and

eyebrows, so she did not need much to make her

beautiful. She had never gotten out of bed the

day before this appointment and was hurting all

over. She was moving slowly and had very little

energy, but managed to get dressed and into the

car. I wondered if the cancer was spreading into

other areas as I saw such a decline in Christy

recently. Having a break from the chemo

seemed like a good idea to let her body rest. *But*

would the disease intensify at a rapid pace

without it? was the question I had in my

thoughts.

~Chapter Twenty Nine~

I sat in the waiting room while Christy

and Corey went back for the scan and fell asleep

because it was so early in the morning. When

they were finished, Christy slowly made it out

and sat for a few minutes to make sure the scan

was successful. She laughed at me sleeping, and

I think she wished she could have curled up

beside me and joined in a little nap. She was

still walking but looked exhausted. Corey pulled

the car up, and we helped her in very carefully to make our way to the hospital to see Dr. Thomas. He had been Christy's oncologist from the beginning, and we were pleased with his expertise and how he treated all of us.

In between the appointments, Christy asked for a smoothie and some food from McDonald's. She had to use the restroom, and we barely made it back to the car with her as the pain was intensifying rapidly. Once in the car, Christy put her head back and shared a story about one of the technicians at the imaging center. She said they told her they had never had a cancer patient be so positive and smiling all the time. I wanted to cry because this touched me and gave me so much bliss. There are no better words than the ones spoken about my children. They are everything to me, and it has always been a blessing to see them praised by others. Just hearing a compliment about them and how they touch others has always been pure joy to this mother's heart. I was so happy that I patted her on the shoulder lightly, but it was much harder than I meant to and Christy began to cry and yell at the same time. I knew she was in pain, but I never realized how much her pain had increased until that moment. I was so upset that I had physically hurt my suffering child. It was a moment that I will carry with me forever. Christy felt awful that she had yelled at me and apologized right away because she was the most forgiving person. This was an extraordinary picture of how Christy's life was lived. She never wanted to hurt anyone, and she was always quick to forgive when someone hurt her. I watched people hurt Christy so badly while she was growing up, and it tore me up every time. Now I had hurt her and could barely breathe. I stared out the car window of the backseat behind Christy and silently cried, wishing I could take back that moment.

When we finally met with Dr. Thomas a few hours later, Christy was really feeling miserable. She wasn't able to use the bathroom, and it was becoming uncomfortable. She had the contrast still in her system, and was unable to eliminate it from her body. The scans were revealed to us, and they were not what we had hoped for. There was a large amount of fluid in Christy's right lung, and the doctor wanted to admit her to have the fluid extracted the next morning. Her blood was too thin to have the procedure immediately, so she would have to be taken off the medication to thicken it up. He also wanted to give her a blood transfusion to build her up. Christy was upset by this and told him she didn't want to stay in the hospital. She just wanted to go home and return the next morning. Dr. Thomas left the room to check on a few things. As the time passed, Christy began to decline rapidly. She realized at that point she needed to be admitted to the hospital. Dr. Thomas was relieved because he really knew deep down what was happening to Christy. He began making the arrangements to find a room for.

It took a long time for a bed to become available, and I knew that Christy would be most comfortable in a private room. I knew she would be very unsettled in a room with others around her. She spoke up quickly asking for the private room, and the doctor said he'd do his best but didn't have much control over that decision. I began to feel a million emotions at that point but tried not to let my thoughts get the best of me.

Christy was becoming more and more nauseous, and she began to vomit. She was getting weak, and it was so hard for her to get comfortable while we waited in the exam room. When the nurse came to tell us a bed was available for her, they let us take her ourselves in the wheelchair from the oncology clinic to the hospital. The room that was ready was on Six Central, Room 48A. I knew when I heard the "A" that it was not a private room. I became very uneasy about how Christy would react to this, but trusted that God would take care of her. Again, the payer I barely whispered would be answered. We began riding up the elevator to the sixth floor, and a pleasant little lady popped in with us about the fourth floor. As the doors closed, she turned to Christy and simply stated, "Jesus is in control." She then exited on the fifth floor while we all just looked at each other. As quickly as she walked into the elevator, she exited, leaving us all with our jaws dropped. The nurse on Six Central greeted us as we stepped out of the elevator and said, "Are you Christy Wright?" We all said yes, and she proceeded to tell us they found a room on Three East, Room 105. My eyes opened wide when I heard her words as I had remembered this was the very room Christy spent all her time in the hospital while waiting for her diagnosis; a private room. Once again, another moment had come when God whispered back to us, "I've got this."

Christ with a y

Once Christy was in bed, her pain
medication was increased to help her relax. It
wasn't helping much and she was drifting in and
out of sleep. I knew that Corey would stay with
her, and felt it was best for me to go home to
take care of Molly. I needed to gather the things
Christy had asked me to bring back for her. She
requested simple things like her glasses, a cell
phone charger, and some clothes. Christy's
vision had changed quite a bit during the
previous year. She was nearsighted, but her
prescription was changing every few months
and she needed her glasses more often than she
had ever needed them before. It seemed to be
another indication that something had been
wrong that we missed.

I left at 6:45 p.m. to get back to
Lynchburg before dark in Christy's little blue

car. This was my first trip driving through the mountains, and I was alone with a heavy heart. I talked with Jeff when I was back in Lynchburg. He wanted to drive back down to be with Christy for her procedure, but I didn't think it was necessary for him to drive all the way back down after just returning home a few days earlier. He decided at the moment to stay home. I could tell he was unsettled as we ended our conversation.

By 11:30 p.m., I was in bed and all was well with Christy. I made sure that everything had been packed for Christy and Molly was taken care of. I would leave early in the morning to go back to the hospital in time for the procedure. I was hopeful that this would be just a small setback and that she would be alright.

~Chapter Thirty~

May 6, 2010 — Morning

At 4 a.m. I was awakened to my phone

ringing, which was unusual, and I was afraid to

answer it. I remember staring at my phone

momentarily with an array of thoughts. When I

answered it, I heard Corey's voice softly

beginning to tell me I needed to come up to the

hospital. The doctors told Corey to call me and

let me know I needed to come as soon as I was able to. When he said Christy didn't want me to, it relieved my fear for a minute. I could hear in Corey's voice that something was very wrong. He had urgency in his words but was doing his best to keep me calm. I stood there feeling like I did the evening we got the call from Corey telling us that they were testing Christy for cancer. I felt numb and weak, but I was pushing myself to function. I was there all alone, knowing I had to get ready and travel ninety minutes to walk into what I knew was going to be agonizing news. I gave myself step by step instructions on what to do before getting behind the wheel of the car. I quickly did everything I needed to do and made sure Molly was fed and let outside. All the motherly instincts kicked in, even for the dog. I got into the car, grabbed the steering wheel with a firm grip, and prayed that

all would be well. It was dark outside and I was

so afraid, but I knew that I would be safe as I

gave my fears to my Savior. As I began making

my way to Charlottesville, I called Jeff to tell

him where I was headed and why. When he

answered, he told me he had just set out on the

road to come down. He wanted to be with us for

Christy's procedure and couldn't sleep, so he

packed up to head down.

I drove through the mountains as fast as

I could, sometimes exceeding the speed limit a

little more than I should have. I couldn't get to

Charlottesville fast enough, but I arrived safely

at 5:45 a.m. and parked in the parking structure

across from the hospital. I walked in through the

all too familiar hallway to get to the lobby,

where I spent many phone conversations with

family and friends. I quickly walked over to the elevator to go up to the third floor. I was met at the door of Christy's room by nurses whisking me into where there was overwhelming activity. They told Christy I was there, and she immediately beckoned for me to come near her. Multiple machines and staff filled the space where Christy laid in pain. She begged me to have them remove the catheter that was necessary because it was causing so much discomfort. The only thing I could do was comfort her with my words and hold her hand. She listened intently to me and kept her focus on me. Corey took me out into the hall and tried to explain to me what had happened and wanted the doctors to tell me what they had told him. Two of the doctors explained to me that they needed to do another CT scan to see what was happening internally. They told me they wanted

to intubate her, but she refused. They explained

the options we had and said there was no right

or wrong answer. The first option described was

to put Christy in Intensive Care on a ventilator

and do what they could to alleviate her pain.

They would do everything they could possibly

do to stop the internal bleeding from the lesions

on her liver that was suspected. The second

option was to heavily medicate her and let her

go. I was in a state of shock at this point and

can't describe the feelings I had that morning. It

was horrifying, to say the least, to be put in this

situation so quickly and unplanned. Corey and I

decided the decisions that would need to be

made would only be done by Christy. She was

now continuously asking for more pain

medication. The medical staff began

administering it to her through the IV as often as she requested it. She was pale and cold to the touch.

The CT scan was ordered and Christy begged them not to do it, but it needed to be done to find the source of agonizing pain she was experiencing. She asked if I could go with her, and I did. I stood in the hall just outside the door. I could not go into the room with her. It was the worst feeling in the world to hear her shrieking as they moved her to the table for the scan. She yelled in agonizing pain through the entire process, and I could hear her through the doors of the room. Once finished, she was taken back to her room where she wanted to be with Corey and me at her side. The staff was looking to put her in intensive care, but she begged them not to for some reason. She was more or less begging to be left right where she was.

I was in awe as to the staff members that God provided us during this experience. There was a doctor just leaving his twelve hour night shift that dropped his bags and came in to help with Christy's care. He was able to comfort Christy in this incredible way that I once again cannot explain. He was gentle, kind, and able to look into Christy's eyes to reassure her that he was there to take care of her. The nurse in charge of her was filled with boundless empathy, and her oncologist was there at her side with tears in his eyes.

The scan showed that there was heavy internal bleeding from Christy's liver. The lesions were basically erupting, and this was why the fluid was accumulating in both lungs now. They began to explain things to Christy, and she was having trouble comprehending the information. She was told again they could intubate her, but she immediately spoke up declining their suggestion. The doctor told her in detail what the options were. Then Corey and I went out into the hallway to talk more with the doctor. He told us the bleeding could be controlled once the breathing tube was inserted, and giving her a blood transfusion would help until more chemo could resume. We knew at this point it would only prolong the inevitable. The other choice was to heavily medicate her and let her go. We told the doctor the choice would be Christy's and we were absolutely convinced we knew what her decision would be.

Corey and I walked into the room where Christy was struggling to breathe and in dire pain. Corey took her left hand and I took her right as we began to tell her what her options were. Corey tried to expel the words we dreaded to utter, and as he was unable to speak, I was given the strength to tell my daughter the decision was hers to make and we would support whatever she chose. Her response was quick and decisive. She told us it hurt too much and she couldn't do it anymore. I told her she didn't have to, and with eyes closed and a big smile she clearly stated what I will never forget: "I get to go to Heaven." Corey and I began to cry, and she told me not to. She told me that I had to proofread Corey's papers until he graduated. She always proofread his work for him, even while she was sick. She turned to Corey and told him that no matter what, he was to finish his degree in the upcoming days. She told us she loved us, and those were the last words she ever spoke.

Corey told her she was the best wife he ever had because we always wanted Christy to smile. I told her she was the best daughter I ever had. We both told her we loved her, and she gripped our hands. They were so cold and I never wanted to let go. I thought about the tiny little hand that gripped my finger almost twenty-five years earlier. The sweet little hand of a toddler holding mine while learning to take her first steps. The hand that grew bigger than mine, but still held it when afraid. I thought about the hands that were held while the vows of marriage were being repeated between husband and wife. The hands that were lifted high while praising Jesus, and folded together while praying precious prayers to Him. We were now holding those beautiful hands that would soon be held

by Christ escorting her into her perfect home.

Two milligrams of Dilaudid were given

to her frequently, as well as Ativan. She had an

oxygen mask on and began calming down. I

went out to call Jeff, my parents, and my sister.

They were all terribly shaken by the news I was

delivering to them in the early hours of that

morning. As I went back down the hall towards

Christy's room, Corey quickly ran out searching

for me. When he found me, he told me he could

sense that the moment was nearing. I was taken

aback as I didn't think she was at that point, and

went right in. Christy was gasping for air and

her eyes were dilated. I grabbed her hand and

sat on the right side of her, and Corey, again sat

on her left, holding the hand that proudly wore

her wedding ring. Patricia, her nurse, began to

whisper in Christy's ear about the Lord and it comforted Corey and me. All the machines were now disconnected from Christy except for her IV. Her breathing was so labored, and she seemed completely unaware of anything, but was still held my hand. At one point I started to let go, and she grabbed it, startling me. A few moments later I watched Christy breathe her last breath at 8:23 a.m. on May 6, 2010.

~Chapter Thirty One~

How do I even explain that moment? It is forever frozen in my mind feeling like a distant memory, and yet as if it happened yesterday. We cried for only a moment and said our good-bye, which was really just a "see you later." What made it sting less for us was the knowledge that Christy was so right. She did go to Heaven. Not because she was a good person or someone who smiled all the time, while introducing herself to complete strangers as the girl who spelled her name Christ with a "Y". She didn't go to Heaven because she cared so much for children, or that she was the sweetest person I had ever known. She went to Heaven because she knew Christ as her Savior, accepted His perfect gift of salvation, and walked each day with Him.

Though she suffered in immense pain while on this Earth during her illness, that is no longer the case. My beautiful Christy has been made whole again, never to suffer another day. She walks in Heaven smiling and praising Christ every single day.

I am grateful to have spent every day with Christy that I was given. She was truly my best friend and the one person with a pure heart that I marveled at. I was given a daughter I could have never imagined receiving. She was a beautiful gift to this world, and I wish everyone could have met her.

~Chapter Thirty Two~

Making the call to Jeff was so painful.

He still had six hours of traveling to do and how

difficult it was for him to drive through tears

and heartache. He pulled to the side of the road,

and together we cried and consoled each other.

Once we finished our conversation, I had to

begin making calls to my family, but I couldn't

call Josh and Ben as I was too heartbroken. I

knew they would take the news hard, and it was better for their dad to tell them.

My first experience with making all the plans and figuring out the details of a funeral was next. Corey and I sat with Christy silently, and then we had to answer many questions. The hospital staff was wonderful, allowing us to spend as much time as we needed with Christy. There were so many people that cared for Christy coming in to see her, and they all cried. After Dr. Thomas became emotional, we could once again see the impact Christy had made on those she met.

Questions needed to be answered, and we began the process of all the plans that would come in the upcoming days. It seemed that it would be a daunting task, but it wasn't. We had the best support, and things fell into place with ease. Christy would be transported from the hospital to a funeral home in Richmond, Virginia, and then flown to Michigan where the funeral would take place.

Patricia said a beautiful prayer with us before we left, and I will forever be grateful for her kindness. She barely knew Christy but seemed to have a love for her. As we walked out of the room, I felt empty and awful. We had always walked out of the hospital with Christy with us, and now we were just leaving her there knowing we wouldn't see her again until days later. As we arrived in the parking structure, the feelings were almost unbearable, and we talked and cried all the way back to Lynchburg.

May 6, 2010 – Afternoon

Christ with a Y

Walking into the little house on Oakdale Drive was so sad. I looked at everything with flashbacks. I thought about all of the exciting work that went into that house to make it a home. The beautiful tree that bloomed with pink and white flowers every spring that drew Christy to buy this house. The hanging baskets that adorned the front porch and the steps that Corey painted because she wanted them to be pretty. I looked at the front door she was so excited that Corey had put in, and the holly bushes that lined each side of the porch.

We sat on the couch together and opened the letter Christy had written to me with her wishes. She told me in the letter that if I were reading it, she would be gone and not to be sad. She asked that we celebrate her life and remember her happy. She asked for a closed casket, beautiful music, which she selected, and a horse drawn carriage to take her to her grave site. She asked to be placed in a vault as opposed to be buried in the ground, and that Pastor Reilly do her service. This is the man she also referred to as "Bud", who had sat with her as she waited to depart for China. After we read the letter, Corey went to their room, and I went down to mine to wait for Jeff.

Caroline and Liz took Molly with them to help alleviate that worry. Jeff arrived in the early afternoon, and we met with paralyzing emotion. I knew by his swollen eyes that he had not stopped shedding tears the entire ride to Lynchburg. We had so much ahead of us but felt like doing nothing as the fatigue from the past few days was setting in. Jeff began to take charge, and we started making phone calls to make as many arrangements as possible before heading back to Michigan.

So many emails began to pour in, and I cried reading every one of them. It was hard being away from home, but at the same time, a good thing because I didn't want to be around anyone. I needed to collect my thoughts and process the loss I had just suffered.

May 6, 2010 – Evening

Corey's best friend never let him down for a minute. He was already on his way down, and Corey went to pick him up from the airport in Charlottesville. The drive back there was not an easy task for Corey, but it was a time he could spend alone wrapping his mind around the devastation he was dealing with. Kelsey would be instrumental in all of what would come in the future and I came to understand this marvelous friendship better than I thought possible.

It was so hard to fathom that earlier in the day I was having a conversation with Christy. I would never be able to call her at the bank and hear her professional voice, with her being disappointed it was only me again and not a new customer. No more deep conversations or ones filled with laughter. No more stories about Corey leaving his socks on the floor or about Molly eating lasagna fresh out of the oven. I would never see her pull out of the driveway honking the horn of the little blue car or hearing crazy songs being sung. There would never be anymore pictures of Christy or vacations spent together on the beach. I would never get to introduce my incredible daughter to anyone again, and it was beginning to sink in. I was

missing her so badly already. What was truly

amazing was how comforted I was; because I

knew that every day that went by would be one

day closer to seeing her again. God's abundant

grace was constant.

~Chapter Thirty Three~

We pulled away from the house on
Saturday, the eighth of May, at 7:20 a.m. with
Jeff in the driver's seat. My husband has always
been a great leader in any situation. Our entire
marriage has been built upon him being the guy
in charge. My time in Virginia taught me how to
be more independent than I have ever been. It
was a good lesson for both of us as it made me
realize how wonderful it has been to be taken

care of so well, but also to prove how the big decisions that had to be made were doable for me. One of the most incredible sayings I have read that made me smile is that, "you never know how strong you are until being strong is the only choice you have." There were so many moments that I had to be strong. There were many situations in which I had no idea that I could possibly muster any more strength, but deep within me, the power of God rested upon me and I persevered.

I could hardly say a word as we left the house on Oakdale Drive in our pick up truck filled with everything we could possibly fit in the bed. Corey and Kelsey were in the back seat of our double cab truck that two fully grown men could barely stretch their legs out in, and I was in the passenger seat. I was fine until we drove by the first apartment complex that Christy and Kimmie lived in when they decided to be independent college girls. I could hold back the emotions no longer and sobbed almost uncontrollably. None of the men in the vehicle knew how to handle my tears and I think we were all a mess. Then all of sudden, as quickly as the tears erupted from my eyes, we were better and began to talk about Christy, laughing and crying intermittently.

Kelsey would also be graduating at the same time as Corey with the same degree, so they stayed up all night finishing homework and writing papers. Most of the trip they slept as the exhaustion caught up with them from the days prior. I knew that Corey was deeply grieving, and his friend was in great pain for the loss Corey was experiencing. Good friends grieve together, and it was evident that Kelsey's heart was shattered in a loving way I had never seen before.

I wrote out the eulogy while traveling, and it surprised me how much I was able to accomplish. This was something I wanted to do because I wanted to honor Christy and talk about the person she was. I could sit for hours and write about my daughter and probably talk to anyone about her for days upon days. The love and smiles she brought to our lives was pretty incredible, and I will never get to a point where I don't want to talk about her. I smile every time I have the opportunity to tell anyone about her life and what it meant to me. The twelve hour ride back to Michigan was long, and my heart ached as my mind was filled with confusion. It is hard to explain the part of me that was lost forever. There is a pain in my heart and a darkness in my mind that will forever be present. I have often heard about people feeling numb when they have lost someone, and that couldn't be any more accurate. Grief is something that consumes the entire body. I was a feeling that I had exploded into hundreds of pieces, and slowly had to pull each of them back into myself. I knew that it would take time to put myself back together, but in those early days, those pieces just drifted away from me.

After our arrival home, it took a long time to unpack everything, but I needed to keep busy. It was so good to be home, but also hard. I wanted to stay home with locked doors. Answering the phone was a chore and most of the time I wanted to avoid it. I knew I needed to keep functioning. I knew that God would hold me close and help me through the heavy weight that was on me. I knew that each of the next few days would be pretty tough, but I was still able to smile and figure out ways that I would honor my daughter's life as we would celebrate it.

The days to follow were consumed with many decisions, all of them I dreaded, but I knew they had to be made.

~Chapter Thirty Four~

Our next trip would be to the cemetery

to choose a spot where Christy would be

entombed. On Monday, May 10th, we went to

Michigan Memorial Cemetery and found a

beautiful spot overlooking the Huron River

facing south. It was at the very top of the

mausoleum, which we chose for specific

reasons. We knew we would be questioned as to

why we chose this spot, but the three of us

agreed it was just where we wanted it. This
place would be peaceful and facing the direction
where her life changed so much. It was the place
she traveled to as a college student ready to take
on a whole new world. A place where she would
turn into an incredible woman of God, find her
calling, and meet her husband. Virginia was
where she began a career, planned her future,
and touched many lives. Oakdale Drive was the
place she set up her home, got to play house for
real, and brought home her puppy. The south
was where she met new friends as a banker and
where she hoped to begin a family. We chose
the top of the mausoleum, not because it was
closer to Heaven as some have speculated, but
for reasons only Jeff, Corey, and I agreed on.

We then went to the viewing, which
began at 1 p.m. Jeff, Josh, Ben, Corey, and I

went in to see her, and she was so pretty and peaceful. Her wedding gown adorned her thin frame; the scarf was placed around her head and braided down her right side. She wore silver earrings and a necklace with a tiny cross. That was appropriate. She was so beautiful that we decided to allow the immediate family, Kimmie, and Kelsey in to see her. It was a good decision as it gave much needed closure for all involved. Some hadn't seen Christy in a long time and others not at all during her illness. It was hard for anyone to visit because Christy was too anxious for company most days.

There were gorgeous red, orange, and yellow gerbera daisies with roses and tulips draped over the casket. We chose them because these were Christy's favorite flowers and the same colors she had chosen for her wedding. I couldn't believe this was us looking at our child,

our relative, our friend, in this situation. It was

such an unnatural feeling for all of us. We didn't

sign up for this. These things happen in movies

or to other people, but not us. To say exactly

how it felt to be there could never be explained.

The desire to run away from the situation was so

prevalent that it would not have taken much for

it to have happened.

As each of the family members entered

the auditorium and walked to the front where we

all were waiting, the obvious signs of sadness

were on each face. The most difficult thing for

me was watching my mom stagger down the

aisle. She was extremely sad and at that

moment, really grasped that her granddaughter

was no longer with us. My mom had just lost

her mother two months prior and had also

experienced the loss of a child. She has always

been good at harboring her emotions, but today

they were loosened and her tears began to flow

down her cheeks. I found myself being strong

for her and trying to talk her through these

moments.

In the next few minutes, I saw Kimmie

walking in all alone. As we met each other's

eyes, I saw the deep sadness in hers, and we met

with hugs and few words. Kimmie had flown up

from her home in Florida to say her goodbye to

Christy and be with us.

The first person to come into the

auditorium after the family time was my teacher

and friend from college, Elaine. When I saw

her, I broke down into tears. I was honored to

see her, and I think everything that was bottled

up inside me let loose. A sea of people began to

flood the aisle leading to the front of the church where Christy was. Flowers were delivered continually, and the exhaustion set in halfway through the day. I couldn't keep my eyes open, nor could I stand anymore. There were so many people, and I just couldn't raise my arms to hug anymore of them. I ended up in a room with my head on a table while close friends and family consoled me.

There were so many people during that time frame that I didn't get to see and I felt terrible, but the exhaustion hit me hard. I made it back out to greet people, but I just wanted to go home at that point. It was so beautiful to see how many people came to support us. My hope was that no one was actually saying goodbye to Christy, but "see you soon." I just kept thinking about the way Christy shared with so many about her faith. My greatest hope was that they would remember her words and how she lived each day. She was so empowered with courage, no matter what she did. It didn't matter how sick she was, how tired she was, or how discouraged she was from things she felt, she still let her feelings about her Savior be known above everything.

Over one thousand people came to say farewell to Christy, and I think that proved that she touched many people throughout her life.

Once the visitation ended at nine, we went home where I became quite sick and eventually went to bed knowing what was to come the next day. As much as I wanted that day to be over, it petrified me all the more. I knew that each day that passed by was one day more that I wouldn't get to hear Christy's voice, see her beautiful blue eyes, or see that gorgeous smile. I had to tell myself that each day that passes is one day closer to when I will see her again. I love the passage in 2 Peter 3:8 (NIV) that says: "But do not forget this one thing, dear friends: With the Lord a day is like a thousand years, and a thousand years are like a day." Those words are great comfort and encouragement for me, and that is how I get through each day.

~Chapter Thirty Five~

The morning of the eleventh came

quickly with rain falling continuously from the

dark sky. We were asked to be at the funeral

service by 10 a.m. for the family to gather. I felt

better from the agony of the previous evening

but was filled with anxiety for what was ahead

of us. The feeling of overwhelming sadness

loomed in the air as we prepared to leave the

house. I can hardly remember getting ready,

every moment seemed to be an eternity. I wore a

simple, black and purple dress with flat shoes

and Jeff wore a typical black suit with a white

shirt and blue tie. The color blue seemed to

always be Christy's color so I understood his

choice.

Corey and I had prepared what we

wished to say about Christy during the days

leading up to the funeral. I remember Corey

finishing his and asking Kelsey to proofread it. I

found Kelsey in our backyard filled with

emotion. He began to talk to me about all that

had transpired during Corey and Christy's short

time together. It was extremely heartbreaking to

see him so upset and only made me realize

again how special the bond was between two

best friends.

The family gathered in the front of the
church surrounded by so many flowers that
were delivered the previous day. More bouquets
were coming in as we stood in front of the silver
casket that was closed and draped with the
beautiful spray of blooms that Christy loved.
We had decided to use the colors of her
wedding which were red, orange, and yellow.
Gerbera daisies were placed everywhere within
the greenery. I can barely remember what they
looked like as I tried to keep my attention off of
this scene. The feeling of being in a dream was
how it all played out for me. I was present yet so
far removed from that day. It was my way of
coping with the sorrow and exhaustion.

Josh had prepared a slide show which
was a tribute of pictures to Christy's life. He
made one to play continuously during the

visitation and one set to music for the funeral.

My favorite photo was put at the end of the

video. It was Christy hugging her dad as he sat

on our back step putting his shoes on to leave.

Her head was on his shoulder as she looked at

the camera. She was only two years old. Josh

had chosen the most appropriate photo to melt

the hearts of all in attendance.

Corey and I had read the letter that Christy had

written to me regarding her wishes if she

someday needed me to know them. I knew that

day I had asked her to write them out was for

the time that was near. Although she was

irritated with me that day, asking her to do such

a thing, I believe she knew why I had requested

her to write out her wishes.

Each request was carefully planned out,

from the songs she asked to be played to the

horse-drawn carriage. I was very pleased

knowing that we did not do anything that

Christy had not asked us to do.

Pastor Reilly came to our home on

Sunday afternoon to go over the service. I felt

that I needed to be in charge and kept my

feelings subdued that day. I wanted to make

sure that I was in the present moment so I

wouldn't miss anything that needed to be done.

I asked that the message given at the funeral

would be all about Christy. I wanted people

attending to know her desire that everyone she

talked to was that they would know Jesus like

she did. I wanted people to think of the way she

was and to remember her for all that she was.

As our meeting came to an end and Pastor

Reilly was on his way out, he made a suggestion

to us. He said the family may want to exit the

auditorium after the funeral service was finished
just before people made their way up to pay
their last respects. He knew there would be
hundreds of people attending the ceremony and
it would take a long time to go through the line
to greet us. We unanimously decided to take his
suggestion.

We also had to visit the funeral home to
choose things that would have to be chosen for
such an occasion. I hated being in that room and
I felt pain and anger for the first time. Not anger
at anyone particular, but a desire to flee. I
wished that I could have ignored everything that
had happened and what was about to take place.
Jeff, once again, was able to stay in charge of
the situation and keep me comforted in a way I
will never be able to explain. The task was

completed and I was happy to have that out of the way.

As people began to come into the church and find their seat, I felt a sense of peace come over me and I stayed at the front of the auditorium near my daughter's casket greeting those who came by. The funeral began promptly at 11 a.m. with Pastor Reilly at the pulpit. He began his opening remarks, and announced that I would be coming up to talk about Christy, and would be followed by Corey. It was still raining and the clouds made the morning feel like evening.

I had written my eulogy on the ride home from Lynchburg and typed it out when I got home. I read it over and over. I knew I could add nothing more. I left the front row to walk up the steps to talk about my best friend, my daughter, my girl. I approached the microphone, stared down at the casket beneath me, and then looked out onto the vast crowd of mourners. I held the sheets of paper with my words printed, placed my elbows on the pulpit to steady myself, and stood on my toes. I barely make the five foot mark in height so I needed to make sure my mouth was close to the microphone as I wanted everyone to hear my tribute to Christy Lynn DePriest Wright. Every word fell from my lips easily and not one tear formed in my eyes. I was so proud and humbled to be able to speak about this beautiful girl that was gifted to me from above. The words of the lady in the elevator just a few days prior echoed in my mind that God was in control. I knew that and always relied on that, but the day she spoke those words was important. God knew I, as well as Corey, needed to hear that in our moment of great despair. He knew what was coming and gave a complete stranger those words to softly speak to us for what was ahead.

Once I stepped away from the pulpit and passed Corey on the way back to my seat, it was his moment to express his thoughts and this is what he said:

Less than three years ago, I stood in this very spot and promised Christy that I would stay by her side until death do us part.
Unfortunately, for reasons beyond what we can comprehend, that time came too soon. I can assure you, today my goal is to say things and handle this situation exactly how Christy would have wanted. That is the goal of me being up

Christ with a y

here, the goal of this entire service . . . to honor Christy.

I'm not sure there is an appropriate message that I can convey to you today; and even if there was, I'm not sure that I would have the strength to do so anyway. So rather than preparing a long, sorrowful eulogy for my wife, I would just like to mention a few special thoughts that I know Christy would have liked me to share. At this time in my life, and for so many of you that cared for and loved Christy, there is really only one place to look to: God and the Bible.

As I began searching for some type of comforting verse or explanation of this past week's events, Romans 8:28 has continuously played in my mind. It states: "And we know that all things work together for good to those who love God, to those who are called

according to His purpose." Since we all know

without a doubt that Christy loved God and was

called according to His purpose, this time in our

lives and the death of my wife will work out for

His good. Though we may not know the when

and the how, or the details of that good, it is a

promise that God has made.

I know for a fact that Christy did not

want her funeral to be sad and sorrowful, but

uplifting and joyful just like she was. If Christy

were here, she would not want any of us to be

sad or tearful. Christy and I based our

relationship off of a policy of honesty. As you

can imagine, this policy got me into trouble on

numerous occasions, but even so, I wouldn't

have changed a thing and I know Christy

wouldn't have either. At no point in our

marriage did we ever hesitate to boldly tell each other the truth.

This policy enabled us not only to have a wonderful marriage, but to have deep, intimate discussions through her last few months of life. Christy and I talked about the possibility of her going to Heaven early. She took great delight in knowing that after her battle with cancer, seeing Jesus would be her next stop.

I can remember our very first date and how for the duration of our meal, Christy spoke the entire time. It didn't even bother me that I didn't do any talking because the way Christy spoke was something I had never experienced before. The date began with me simply asking her to tell me about herself. I was expecting a traditional response of a few details of her life, but rather for the next half hour, with a huge smile on her face, she told me about her belief in God, her love for missions, and her love for people. From that moment forward, I knew Christy was someone special. Never had I met a person more radiant regarding their faith and love for everyone. I often feel that this set the tone for our entire marriage. I found myself, many times, being more and more impressed at the amount of passion, love, and faith that Christy had.

One of our favorite sayings was, "it's only temporary." This would often help us get through a tough homework assignment, a long line at McDonald's, or a traffic jam filled with inadequate Virginian drivers. Although this statement may seem small, I've often felt that this is exactly how Christy lived her life. She understood that there is a beginning and an end to life. She understood that what you do on this earth is only temporary; the real party is in Heaven.

As I shared earlier, honesty was always our policy, and I will continue to carry that with me for the rest of my life, especially today. Christy would want nothing more than for each and every person in this room to have the same outlook on life that she did. This doesn't happen by chance and would require much effort on your part. Christy understood that her Father in Heaven is just and holy. Christy also understood that as humans, we are unjust and unholy. Christy knew that Jesus was the only answer for bridging the gap between an eternity in heaven or an eternity in Hell. Christy knew that knowing Jesus and living for Him was the best decision anyone can make in their life.

The Story of Christy DePriest Wright

I want people today to leave this place having the same peace about the end of life as Christy did. I truly feel blessed and honored to have been the husband of Christy Lynn, and I would like to end with a quote of Christy's that truly illustrates her outlook on life.

"I believe in smiling. I really do. Sometimes I get mean stares or rolled eyes, but you know what? You never know what just happened to the person behind you in the checkout line at Walmart or the little old guy walking into the bank next to you. You don't know if their spouse just died or if they just found out they have cancer. A smile won't make the world better, but it surely can give someone a little hope. After all, if Jesus were standing next to me in line at Walmart, I KNOW He would smile at me..."

Christ with a y

"I want to leave a legacy. How will they remember me?"[1]

The room was silent when Corey finished and left his position, heading to his seat in the front pews where all of us sat together. We shared a quick smile and looked to Pastor Reilly as he made his way up the stairs to begin speaking. He fashioned his service into words of hope and told the story of Christy's testimony. As he began speaking, he melted into tears and then blamed me for not allowing him to go first. He talked about how Liberty University builds champions and that Christy was a champion for Christ. As soon as he said that, he could not contain his tears. At that moment, I knew how

---

[1] This was a quote from a song by Nicole Nordeman that Christy lived by. An artist that Christy loved.

special Christy was to everyone that knew her.
That smile drew people to her, and just being
near her made it obvious that she was unique
and beautiful. She prayed for people she knew
that needed prayer. She gave what she had to
others and helped people through dark times.
Christy was so young yet filled with so much
wisdom: wisdom she sought from the Lord,
endlessly. Her Bible looked like it belonged to
someone who lived many years, filled with
notes and highlighted scripture.

Her favorite songs that she had chosen
were played after all the words were spoken.
The flood of pictures played on the big screens
at the end that Josh had so carefully put together
with music. I saw both of my sons cry for the
first time during this whole ordeal, and it made
my heart sadder than it already was. Watching

my mom, "Grandma Janet," fall apart drew a pit in my stomach. I had become a different person at this point trying to stay strong for everyone. I knew where it came from, and I depended on it completely. It was not easy watching the grief fall over the many people in the auditorium. I could hear it, I could see it, and I could feel it. I could only think about what was to come next. I operate this way in general, but this was the way I had been coping with everything since Christy had become ill less than a year ago.

As the people began to leave the church to go to the cemetery, it started to rain harder than it had been earlier. Very special young men were asked to be pallbearers. They were people that were special to Christy. There were more people in Christy's life that she thought highly of, but we only needed six. We chose a brother-in-law, a best friend, and four young men that had a special friendship with Christy throughout her years. I'm sure they never expected to be in this position, but they did it without hesitation. Christy had a special ability to make anyone in a room feel like they were part of the crowd. There were many times in her Sunday School class that she made sure the person in the back row felt welcome. She was able to mingle with everyone in a group wherever she was. No one ever felt alone when Christy was around. One of the young men that were asked to be part of this day was away at college. I had sent Anderson a text asking him to be a pallbearer because Christy had a special friendship with him. He was a few years younger than she was. They had been to The Bahamas together on a mission's trip through the youth group and built a sweet relationship. Without hesitating, Anderson said he would be there. I later found out that he left school to fly home at the end of the semester to do what he had been asked to do. I cried when I found out how he so selflessly honored Christy that day.

We made our way to the cemetery, and Christy was taken to her resting place by a horse drawn carriage. Final words were spoken under a pavilion. Then, we walked in the pouring rain to where her casket would be lifted into the highest place in the area we had chosen just a few days prior to this sad event. Everyone that followed us here watched in silence, and flowers were placed in a vase from the service. Corey and I chose the ones we thought were most beautiful and they were placed in the front of the door of the crypt. Her name, and the year

Christy Lynn Wright 2010, was etched into the stone with the flower. It was a sight no parent or young husband wanted to see, but it was a reality we had to accept. As we drove away, knowing this part of a beautiful story was ending, I let my thoughts reflect on what was next. I knew where my daughter was, and that gave me a great sense of peace and hope.

There were so many cards to open after everyone left our home. We invited family and close friends over for lunch as we knew we needed to just finish out the day with people that were a part of Christy's life. Once everyone left and the food was cleaned up, we had to go and pick up the flowers from the service. I was in no place to make any decisions, so I asked that all the flowers be brought to our house. I had no idea how many bouquets there were and our home turned into a floral disaster, but it was

good to see all the love that had poured in

through kind hearted friends.

A memorial service was held for Christy

in Forest, Virginia, for all of the friends and co-

workers who could not attend her funeral in

Michigan. Liz and Caroline, from the bank,

made a recording of the service and sent it to us

later on with all the cards and letters people had

written. Once again, they had both gone above

and beyond for us, and we will forever be

grateful to them. Their friendship to Christy was

genuine shown through the way they cared for

her deeply while she was sick. These two

women cared deeply for Corey and Christy

showing them so much compassion. They also

extended that to me in more ways than I can

express.

Corey left with his parents to travel back to Lynchburg. He would be graduating with his MBA that weekend. Everything was going by so quickly at that moment because Corey and I had been with each other every day for months. We endured so much heartbreak together watching Christy suffer and pass away in front of us. There was no time to adjust with the busyness of life. I didn't know what to do to move forward, and I knew I was in no condition to travel back to Virginia at the time to be there for his graduation ceremony. Part of me wanted to, but I was too exhausted and torn between the two places. I had been away from all that was familiar for a long time and the desire to stay home to be with my husband and boys was what I needed most.

Christ with a y

I was so excited the day Christy was
born and I heard that she was a girl. I had a boy
and a girl, not knowing what future children
God had in store for us. Christy was a beautiful
baby with fuzzy, flaxen hair and the prettiest
blue eyes. Watching her dad hold her and
quieting her were charming memories. She grew
into a woman I absolutely adored and will miss
immensely. She left this world with the same
fuzzy, blonde hair and stunning blue eyes. I sat
and thought about the phone calls and millions
of emails would be no more, and how I will
never hear her tell me she loves me again on this
earth.

I am grateful for the twenty-four years,
eleven months, and twelve days that I had with
Christy. She was able to do all the things she
wanted to in her short life, except to have a

child of her own. I know that hurt her because she mentioned it often while she was sick, which brought tears to her eyes every time. I often wish she would have been able to have had a child before she became ill. I would have been able to catch a glimpse of her through that child. To dwell on such things is not my style though. I know that God's plans are higher than mine, and His way is perfect. That is where I choose to keep my thoughts and gain my strength each morning when I get up. There is no greater plan than the one our God designs for us!

~Chapter Thirty Six~

On the fourteenth of May, 2010, Corey
was on the football field of Liberty University
receiving his Master's Degree in Business. He
had worked for the university, and they had
received word of Christy's passing. During the
opening statements of the graduation ceremony,
Corey was asked to stand, and his story was told
of his loss. I'm sure he was inundated with
emotion at that moment but held it all in. We

were so proud of Corey, knowing how difficult it was for him to finish his studies with all that had happened throughout that entire year. Christy had an itinerary of what she dreamed of in a husband, and having a degree was on that list. It was important to her, and Corey made sure it happened as he loved her so much.

I was always in awe that my daughter had hefty goals and big dreams for her life. I loved even more that she waited on the Lord to show her what He had for her life. Christy never wavered from her morals and convictions. When she was dating Corey, she prayed constantly that he was who God had planned to be her husband. I watched her cautiously fall in love with her gift from God, but I was amazed at how she fell more deeply in love with him weeks before they were married.. The promises they made to each other never ceased. The vows were taken seriously by both of them, which is, "To have and to hold from this day forward, for better, for worse, for richer, for poorer, in sickness, and in health, until death do us part."

I'm sure that we all, as married couples, have promised these words, or something similar, to each other, but have we really thought about them and taken them completely seriously? Christy and Corey experienced each of these promises during their short marriage. There were many better days that overshadowed the difficult days. Their marriage was filled with richer days with their love over the poorer ones. The sickness that came over the health ended in their parting by death. There is no way they uttered these promises on that summer day in 2007 knowing what was ahead of them.

Corey began to sell everything immediately, Molly went to live with Caroline and Spencer, and the little house on Oakdale Drive was put on the market. He moved to Wisconsin with Kelsey and his wife just days after graduation wanting to start over far from Virginia. I knew it was a difficult decision and a quick one, but I also knew how distraught he was. A trailer was filled with what little Corey didn't sell. Things he knew belonged to Christy were brought to me en route to his new home with his best friend. I was so happy to see him and moved that he thought to bring me all that he had.

Corey brought things to me that he couldn't part with, but also knew he couldn't keep with him. He knew they would be treasured by me, and he was right. Every little

thing that Christy had taken with her from our
storage closet at home came back to us. I went
through everything he brought to me. All of her
childhood things she had saved were in the
containers. Some things made me laugh while
others made me cry. The thoughts of who I
would pass these things down to sent me into a
river of tears. I could hear the words being said
at her birth: that my baby was a girl. I prayed
for a healthy baby and was elated that I had
children. I thought about the unique relationship
I had with my mom and dreamed I would have
that with my daughter. God blessed me with that
prayer, and I was so happy. I thought about how
my mom cared for her mom as she aged and
then thought about my daughter not being there
for me as the aging process would set upon me
one day.

I organized and packed all the memories away. I displayed some of her favorite pictures that sat out in her living room on the bookcase that Corey had made for her. I put the sapphire ring I had gotten her on her sixteenth birthday on my finger next to my wedding ring. I knew it would be a daily reminder of Christy's smile.

I not only was grieving the loss of my girl, but I was seeing the broken heart of my son-in-law. We talked on the phone every day and sent texts whenever we needed to. Although we had lost the same person, we had lost a completely different relationship. We both understood that and worked on lifting each other up when we needed to. Some days were harder for me to get through and on those days, Corey was doing a little better. The opposite was almost always ongoing. We were always ready to help each other through every day. I was so glad to have that friendship with Corey and can't imagine how we would have ever been able to get through those dark days without each other.

There were many places I would go where my heart seemed to sag inside my chest. It could go directly into a different mood quickly and just stay there. The best way to describe that feeling was to think about looking up to the sky and seeing a white cloud continue to billow across with the sun shining on it. Then seeing the beauty against the blue sky as it floats through the air. Then a dark blue mass of water vapor blowing gently in front of that sunshine-filled cloud, filled with a vast amount of water just waiting to break free and spill out on the earth unable to hold the contents no more.

The Story of Christy DePriest Wright

~Chapter Thirty Seven~

Christy looked to Corey for comfort, and he never let her down. He was always by her side through the days, weeks, and months of her illness. Corey spent every night with her sleeping on an uncomfortable hospital sofa at Lynchburg General Hospital. There was a rollaway bed of sorts for him to sleep on at The University of Virginia Hospital. Never once did he complain about anything. I know that each day he had to go to work was a struggle. Corey

wanted to be with Christy every day as he knew

they were numbered. Only God knew the

amount of days left in her life on this Earth.

Each day was a gift and even on the hardest

days, we knew how blessed we were to have her

with us.

Corey and I promised to stay in constant

contact with one another. I knew that living with

Kelsey and Ashley would be healing for my

son-in-law, but I sensed that he would struggle

with a great deal of grief. He pushed himself

hard in the weeks that followed the funeral,

waiting for the ache in his heart to be relieved.

That did not happen, and Corey was suffering a

great deal. He found himself unable to keep a

job for very long as reminders of his time with

Christy crept up on him. There were many

important conversations between the two of us as the months went by. Conversations about the raw emotions we were dealing with. There were questions along with pinning blame on things as to how this could have happened. Was it a medication that caused the cancer or was it a doctor's misdiagnosis? We didn't know nor will we ever, but it was something that had to be discussed. Our only conclusion was that we needed to be at peace with it and know that Christy had beautifully lived the life she was given. Of course, we still had questions, but we have never blamed God, we have trusted Him fully with the plan only He had designed for Christy. From the moment she was conceived, God knew the number of days she would walk on this earth.

The summer months were filled with
emotions for me as each day brought its own
new feelings. Sometimes the air felt heavy, and
other days I was able to smile. We began
piecing our lives back together, weaving it into
a new sense of normal. Trying to figure out how
to answer the questions we were asked, and how
to deal with unpleasant conversations with
people. An entire new way of watching movies
and television advertisements hit us like a ton of
bricks. It had never crossed my mind before
how a commercial could be centered on an
event that had just happened in life. Whether it
was a commercial about a funeral home, a
hospital, or the topic of cancer, it would pull
Jeff and me right back to the pain.

Locking eyes with someone I had not
seen since the funeral was exasperating. I

wanted to smile without saying a word because sometimes the tears would fall before I could speak. A song would melt my entire being, and I would be swallowed up by the lyrics. I will never be able to thank the people in my life for how much love they expressed to us. There would be cards in the mail every day for weeks, and gifts waiting for me at my front door. My phone would ring with calls from concerned family and friends, but I could not answer them. My sweet husband was always keeping a close eye on me and doing exactly what I needed him to do without saying a word. He knew when to smile at me and when to wrap his arms around me. He also knew when to walk away, so I could pull myself together. I knew he needed me as much as I needed him, but he was so strong, and he continued to be the steady and strong rock he had been in the months prior to Christy's death.

What seemed to ease my pain and help me heal were the conversations I was able to have with people about Christy. I wanted to talk about her continually. I was able to smile whenever she was talked about. Friends of Christy that I had never met would send me cards or emails about her and how she had impacted their lives. They would share stories about their funny, compassionate friend. These were the things I treasured and began to focus on rather than the emptiness of her being with us no longer.

She was a sassy little girl who fell in love with her dad at the beginning of her life and eventually became my best friend. Christy loved everyone around her as much as she was able to. When she made the recording of only a few of the questions Kelsey's mom had prepared, she told about her love for the people she was surrounded by most. She made me laugh when she talked about how she loved dancing with me as a little girl and how her Grandma Janet's baking always woke her senses. I love that I can still play that tape whenever I want to hear her voice. I wish the rest of the questions on that paper could have been answered, but Christy was too tired to finish them. She is with her Heavenly Father now, at peace. I can picture her beaming face praising the Lord without ceasing for eternity. For me to be sad about that is quite the contrary. I will always physically miss my girl, but my hope is in my Savior who will one day bring me to that same place. I know that for sure, because like Christy, I have accepted Him and have been given the gift of salvation.

~Chapter Thirty Eight~

Christy's Legacy of Hope

Early in 2011, we were approached by a coworker and friend of Christy's at Texas Roadhouse. She thought it would be appropriate to hold an annual event in honor of Christy to raise money for anything we thought Christy would have liked. We were so thrilled and knew we needed to figure out where the funds would go. During this thought process, we tossed around a few ideas, and we decided to begin a non-profit charity in Christy's memory that benefitted orphaned children. We wanted to include Christy's name, so we chose, "Christy's Legacy of Hope," because this lovely lady had left an incredible legacy filled with hope. Our hope would be to try and do just a little of what Christy may have done, had she been given more days in this life. Since that was not God's plan for our daughter, we felt God was leading us to fulfill her dream.

By April of that same year, everything was legally put into place, and we were given the right to a 501(C)(3) non-profit charity organization to do what we could for the orphaned children throughout the world. We really did not have a clue as to how this would play out but trusted God would lead us to where He wanted us. Corey was instrumental in starting our new organization, helping with many details as well as financing the start-up fees.

Our first event was held at Texas Roadhouse, and it was an amazing event. We raised more money than I could have ever imagined. Corey was able to attend which made it all the more special. A local television reporter stopped by to find out what we were all about. The interview was aired later that evening giving us some much needed recognition. We would continue this annual event with a different theme each year. Whether it has been a cowboy theme or nautical, it has been interesting to see the response. We have included a bake sale that has been one of the best ideas, bringing in all kinds of funds. People have been so generous with their donations to this organization. People who loved Christy volunteer to help with the events or whatever our needs are. We hold a variety of fundraisers throughout the year, and whatever we raise, we use to help children in many countries. China, India, Haiti, Sierra Leone, Mexico, and the Philippines are a few places that have benefitted. We have most recently been blessed to work with our local area doing things for children in foster care.

Christy had a wonderful friendship with a family in Lynchburg. Not long after we started Christy's Legacy of Hope, I received an email letting me know that this family had moved to a new location. Professor Gerdes had accepted a new position at another college. He told me a story of how he was speaking of Christy to a colleague, telling him about her aspirations. The colleague mentioned a young lady he knew with a similar heart for orphans. Her name was Katie, and she would soon be traveling to volunteer in an orphanage in China. In the email was information on how I could contact Katie, and I immediately wrote to her.

Katie told me all about her story, the reason she had such a great passion for the fatherless, and how excited she was to travel. She also told me about a young lady that lit this fire under her for the children Christy so badly wished to serve. I was then introduced to a young woman named Autumn. I could hardly wait to contact Autumn and hear her story. I knew that God was connecting the dots, and my heart was thumping in my chest just thinking about what would soon play out.

Autumn and I began talking to each other and listening to our backgrounds of being Christ followers, our desire to work with orphaned children, and adoption. She was so much like Christy. She was a young college student just a few years behind Christy with a heart as big as ever. She had already been to several orphanages in China to work and I later found out her mother had adopted several children. Well, a whole bunch of children. God had led me to someone that would become a huge part of my life. Autumn would also help me do amazing things for Christy's Legacy of Hope. This would eventually be the link to working with the largest Chinese adoption agency in the United States, Chinese Children Adoption International (CCAI).

I was able to send a huge list of things to Autumn to take to the orphanages with her on her long trip. She was incredibly fun and easy to work with, and I built a magnificent amount of trust in our friendship. We talked on the phone all the time, and she connected me with the adoption agency I now work with diligently.

CCAI is located in Colorado, and I was able to contact Xia, the Charity Project Director, with Autumn's assistance. This sweet woman has become like a sister to me and our friendship, as well as our work relationship, has grown immensely over the past five years. She has connected me with orphanages in the area where they work in China to fulfill wish lists for these places. I began sending things but the expense led me to do other things to be more economical. When the list is given to Xia, she contacts me to let me know the need and if possible, it is taken care of. Christy always wanted to make the world a better place by caring for the little ones that needed love and care. This organization was beginning to make me smile and know that I was given a large pair of shoes to fill by my daughter.

I know I will never be able to do the things that Christy was capable of, but every little thing God entrusts me with is a moment of happiness for me. I know the blueprints for our lives have been laid out long before our existence on this Earth. I know that Christy's life was exactly how it was planned, and I am eternally grateful for the years Christy was here to impact so many people. I find it completely

honorable to carry on her legacy.

I promised I would always wait for

God's whisper in my ear when He wanted to

move forward with anything through this

charity, and He continues to give me more than

I could ever ask for.

He has shown me areas in the world,

other than China, that are in need. Whatever He

has given me to do, I have always tried to do it,

and it never ceases to amaze me that there are

always funds to provide what is needed.

Eventually, I was able to host a beautiful

gathering along with CCAI. Families from all

over the Midwest came to my hometown to see

what Christy's Legacy of Hope was all about

and meet Joshua Zhong, co-founder of CCAI,

and his sister, Xia — whom I requested to

come. I witnessed a barrage of families walk through the doors with beautiful children they had adopted. Autumn and her mom traveled as well to be part of this special event. We were able to share our stories and chat with all the people that came. I was in total awe of what happened that day, and it gave me an even bigger desire to work harder at what I was given.

Annually, to raise funds for this work, we host a golf outing and other events. It is still a somewhat small charity, but it is just where God wishes it to be. It isn't about being big or well-known because that is not what Christy would have wished for.

Everything from what Christy's Legacy of Hope does for orphaned children to what we hope to accomplish in the future can be found

on the web-site at: christyslegacyofhope.com

~Chapter Thirty Nine~

A few years later, Corey was introduced

to someone who lived in Iowa. She was seven

hours away from where Corey lived in

Wisconsin. He began having phone

conversations with this young woman named

Deanna. I began hearing more and more about

this girl who Corey was traveling on the

weekends to visit. I loved that Corey kept me in

the loop of his new life. He eventually informed

me that he was going to ask this tall, blonde

woman to be his wife. He had already brought

her to our house to meet us and I couldn't help

but love her right away. The only rough patch I

had with this was seeing the first picture Corey

sent me of the two of them dancing together. It

made me cry tears of sadness and tears of joy all

at the same time.

My favorite words that Corey said to me

when he told me his plans to marry Deanna

were that she wasn't a replacement but an

addition. He couldn't have spoken more words

of truth when he said that. She was absolutely

wonderful and Jeff and I accepted Deanna into

our family with great joy.

We traveled with my parents to Iowa for

the wedding in late May of 2012. Many people

had their opinions but my heart knew it was

right. The ceremony began and Corey would glance over at me occasionally as if to say it would all be good. I watched him make those promises to Deanna and knew he would keep them as long as they both should live. I glanced over at the little boy who had been a ring bearer at Corey's marriage to Christy who was now singing a song at his marriage to Deanna. I watched friends standing up with Corey and Deanna as witnesses to the vows and love between a new couple. I kept my mind from wandering and I was fine throughout the duration of the ceremony.

Music is always the trigger and at the reception, it took one song for me to lose my composure. It was rough and I wasn't able to stay any longer, but that was okay. Everyone understood and I was thankful to have had the honor to be at this event.

To this day, Corey and Deanna are a vital part of our lives. We try to travel together as often as work schedules will allow and we talk or text almost every day. Deanna has definitely become an addition to our family just as Corey said and we have been extremely blessed to have her as our daughter-in-law. It's always fun to introduce them as our son and daughter-in-law when we are all together.

Corey now holds a great position with a company and resides with Deanna near his best friend, Kelsey and his wife Ashley. Deanna has helped Corey heal and has become an incredible friend to me. We share many conversations that are filled with laughter and sometimes tears. I am able to share my love for Christy with her and her story as well. Deanna was such a blessing from God for both Corey and myself because she walked into so much heartache and journeyed through it with tenderness.

God has given us so much grace and without Him, we would have fallen to pieces easily. He has bonded us all together and created an extended family with so much strength. It is never easy and some days the strength refuses to bring us out of sadness but we know that God will shine through the dark days.

~Chapter Forty~

Christy Lynn DePriest Wright was born on a warm sunny day on the twenty fourth of May in 1985. Her fuzzy little head and blue eyes caught the attention of her dad and he held her tight, quieting her soft cry. The little girl I knew would one day take care of me when I grew old had entered the world in the early morning hours. I couldn't wait to put her in pretty dresses with lace and matching hair bows.

She was only seven pounds ten ounces and I had no clue in those moments of meeting her that she would become the incredible woman with bigger plans than imaginable. This baby girl would go from being fussy and sassy to a young lady that wore a smile well. Her words lifted others when they were down and introduced them to Jesus. Her heart was huge and she gifted many with love. Her time on this earth may have been short but she didn't waste a minute of it.

Our beautiful daughter was given to us for just shy of twenty-five years and I am so thankful that we loved her to the fullest of our ability. I'm so glad we spoiled her with the things we did and that she never took anything we did for her for granted. I'm glad she was blessed with two brothers to love her and show her how to be tough. She was placed in the middle of the birth order between Joshua and Benjamin playing her roles of big and little sister well. A piece of us is missing each in a different way. We lost a daughter, a sister, a granddaughter, a niece, a wife, a friend, and a sister in Christ. Nothing will ever fill that emptiness in our hearts because grieving never ceases and can only be felt when we love someone. Christy was loved by many people and those that didn't know her tell me often they wish they could have met her.

There is a place that has been prepared for us where Christy is and that comforts us when we think about Christy. We are certain that she is safe in the arms of our Lord and we will see her again. That is the hope we have because of the cross and that is the message that Christy conveyed to anyone she met.

I'm really glad I sat at the dining room table on May 23, 1985 to write out the many ways to spell the little girl's name I was about to give birth to. How beautiful those letters all looked on that piece of paper when I saw them spelling Christy. You know, the girl who told people her name was spelled Christ with a "y".

Let not your heart be troubled: ye believe in God, believe also in me.

In my Father's house are many mansions: if it were not so, I would have told you. I go to prepare a place for you.

And if I go and prepare a place for you, I will come again and receive you unto myself; that where I am, there ye may be also.

Christ with a Y

And whither I go ye know, and the way ye know.

I am the way, the truth, and the life: no man

cometh unto the father but by me.

~John 14: 1-4 & 7

Acknowledgement

Writing this book was an idea that came to me almost immediately after the events that took place in May of 2010. I knew in doing so it would be healing and heartbreaking. The healing took place after realizing what had been accomplished through the life of a true champion for Christ. The heartbreak came with tear filled eyes thinking about all that had transpired while writing each chapter of this book. I am forever grateful to the God of creation who gave me a precious gift for just shy of twenty-five years. It was a true blessing to be chosen as the mother of a vivacious girl named Christy Lynn.

There would have been no possible way for this story to have been told without the many people in my life that encouraged me to write it. My husband, Jeff, went through many of the same emotions as I did as well as his own struggles. He was and always has been a loving husband and dad to his family. He kept me together when I was falling apart and made his daughter smile when she was scared.

A great amount of love and thanks go to my two strong, wonderful sons, Joshua and Benjamin for supporting me in this journey. I know it has been very difficult on them to listen to me constantly talk about their sister. The love they had for her was immeasurable and even though they don't verbalize it, I know in my heart they miss her. I love them both.

My parents, Julius and Janet Enesey are to be thanked for being the most loving and supportive people in my life. They both encouraged me in everything I have ever set out to do and it continued with their grandchildren. The love they pour into them is extraordinary. They have always believed in me and given me the best direction in following my dreams.

Corey Wright is the strongest and most courageous young man that I have ever had the privilege to know. He endured so much pain and sadness at such a tender age. He made the promise of forever to his bride and kept it through every agonizing day. Sleepless nights and days of uncertainty never kept him away from Christy's side. I am grateful to Corey for many things including his confidence that this story would be told. I'm happy he found love again and that we have become a family.

There are many friends that Christy had to walk through life with. Her very best friend,

Kimmie Tuley was the one who will always stand out. Thank you for being the most beautiful friend to Christy. Always laughing and being by her side through everything. I am grateful for all the timelines and stories you shared with me to write about all the college day shenanigans.

Without the wonderful friends, Caroline McDonald and Liz Royer, we would have never been able to get through some of the roughest days in Lynchburg. From grocery shopping, homemade dinners, and paying kennel bills to taking care of Molly with walks and play dates. Your love for Christy was amazing and your friendship outstanding. You have been instrumental in this story with your passion.

I am indebted to A.J. Reilly for his dedication and expertise in what went into this project. The amount of time and energy he put into this was above anything I ever expected. The friendship he and Christy had made him the obvious person for me to go to for direction. Thank you, A.J., for the talent you provided and guidance in the publishing of this story.

There are many beautiful friends that helped make this book possible and I am grateful for all of you. Corrine, Allie, and Jared, thank you for supplying your editing skills. Taylor Illgen for using your talents to create an incredible cover for me. Laura for the support and love you filled me with, and to Pastor John Reilly for your leadership and friendship to our family.